# The Unsolved Murder of
# a U.S. Citizen by China (Taiwan)
# C.I.A. in U.S.A.

# The Unsolved Murder of a U.S. Citizen by China (Taiwan) C.I.A. in U.S.A.

## The Murder of Henry Liu

*GEORGE K. F. WANG, PhD*

Writers Club Press
San Jose  New York  Lincoln  Shanghai

**The Unsolved Murder of a U.S. Citizen by China (Taiwan) C.I.A. in U.S.A.**
The Murder of Henry Liu

Writers Club Press
an imprint of iUniverse, Inc.

For information address:
iUniverse, Inc.
5220 S. 16th St., Suite 200
Lincoln, NE 68512
www.iuniverse.com

ISBN: 0-595-14907-3

Printed in the United States of America

# Statement Of Purpose

The happening of Henry Liu's murder was no accident. It was an incident resulting from years of upheaval in Chinese political history. Henry was a humble man who lived the quiet life of a scholar with his wife and children in San Francisco. If so, why was he murdered?

This book analyzes the historical elements of Henry's murder, his involvement with the Kuomintang, and the nefarious ways in which the Taiwanese secret police have infiltrated America. It is my intention that American readers who are unfamiliar with Chinese ways and customs will be inspired by this book, especially when observing the present crisis and mounting tensions between the U.S. and mainland China.

Americans have become increasingly alarmed by revelations of missile defense espionage by Chinese scientists, the Clinton campaign finance scandal, the bombing of the Chinese embassy by NATO forces in Yugoslavia, and the unabated human rights abuses of Tibetans. A Pentagon report to Congress in March 1999 details a sharp increase in the deployment of Chinese missiles against Taiwan, fueling calls in the United States for the development of the Theater Missile Defense system to protect U.S. forces in the event of a war.

These two core issues-China's human rights record and American policy toward Taiwan—have long been the most contentious issues in the often-difficult relationship between the nations. Within the pages of this book, readers will come to a new understanding of Chinese reasoning, history and politics: a full disclosure of Taiwan's false democracy, indifference to international law, and the unique cooperation between gang lords and the highest levels of Taiwanese government. And, as Taiwan continues to plead for U.S. aide and intervention, the reader will ultimately understand the folly of intervention in Chinese political affairs.

Henry Liu was born in Mainland China. He was a highly respected and controversial news columnist. He immigrated to the United States from Taiwan and became a U.S. citizen, continuing to earn his living as a commentator on Chinese politics. He published a book, and that book cost him his life. The shocking aspect of his murder was not that he was gunned down on the streets of Taipei—where such occurrences are commonplace-but that foreign agents assassinated him in his home near San Francisco.

Imagine waking up one morning and hearing the news that Rush Limbaugh or David Halberstam or some other writer had been murdered pursuant to publishing a book about Bill Clinton, that a citizen of the United States was killed for exercising his right of free speech. Imagine the outrage, the ensuing investigation, the arrests and trials.

Why, then, has the reader probably never heard of Henry Liu?
This is Henry's story. This is how it happened.

# *A Background To Chinese Political History*

The Republic of China (ROC) was founded by Sun Yixian (Yatsen) in 1912. His Chinese National People's Party, commonly referred to as Nationalists, espoused the Three People's Principles of Nationalism, Democracy and Economic Reform. Once in power, the Nationalists became known as the Kuomintang (KMT).

After Sun's death in 1925, Jiang Jieshi (Chiang Kai-Shek), commandant of the Soviet-financed Whampoa Military Academy, launched a military drive against the warlords, moved the KMT capital to Nanjing from Canton, and seized Beijing. Jiang proclaimed loyalty to Sun's principles, which he built into his Confucianist New Life Movement, in 1934. Jiang was married to Sun's U.S.-educated sister-in-law, and was further influenced by western thought by embracing Methodism.

Jiang's unification of Mainland China did not last long. Mao Zedong, founding member of the Chinese Communist Party, broke with the KMT in 1927, and was driven from the cities to a bleak outpost in the great Northwest. Here Mao evolved the guerilla tactics of the "people's war," attacking remote areas too far from the cities for the KMT to effectively protect.

In 1934, Jiang's KMT virtually destroyed Mao's base of operations, followed by the Long March which saw 100,000 Communist forces retreat to Shanxi to set up a new base. Two years later, under increasing threat of Japanese invasion, Jiang renewed an alliance with Mao that not only established Mao's supremacy in the Communist party but also restored his former power.

With the Japanese invasion of China in 1937, Jiang was forced to move the KMT capital to Chongqing. The Japanese occupation lasted until

1945, whereupon Mao took advantage of the KMT's weakened condition and waged a civil war lasting four years.

Jiang's regime was ousted from the mainland, and he retreated to Taiwan with 2 million refugees and 500,000 troops, where, under U.S. military protection, he maintained hostility to Mao's new People's Republic that continues today.

Jiang's nationalist government in Taiwan was comprised of a national assembly of 920 members and a parliament of 313 members. Jiang, as president, appointed a premier and a president of the Executive Council, who served at his pleasure.

In 1978, Jiang Jieshi's son, Jiang Jingguo (Chiang Ching-Kuo), became Taiwan's president. The son had risen in the ranks as his father's prime minister for all of one year, then as president of the Executive Council for seven years. As the nation's leader, Jiang Jingguo's most important accomplishment was continuing a lasting relationship with the United States, without whom the "renegade province" would quickly lapse under mainland control. And in order to maintain that most valuable relationship, Taiwan must at all times appear to be the vision of democracy and economic reform we publicly held out ourselves to be, a nation that celebrates freedom and human rights above all else. At least, that is what the KMT would have everyone believe.

Billions of American dollars have poured into Taiwan and will continue to flow as long as Taiwan plays by the rules. Much of the humanitarian aide has never reached its intended beneficiaries: the hundreds of millions of dollars earmarked for Taiwanese veterans' pensions in return for providing a first line of defense against mainland China has been routinely skimmed by the higher echelons of the KMT. While veterans and their families starve in the streets, the government of Taiwan maintains one of the largest reserves of U.S. currency in the world.

# *PROLOGUE*

27 March 1991

Wind chime chattering. The hum of mumbled mantras. Incense smoke swirling. Candles glow on an altar. Green tea brews in a clay pot.

With the ringing of a tiny silver bell, the séance begins. The medium, Madame Chu, has been called to the home of Jung-Tsi Tsui, who claims she is haunted by the spirit of her murdered husband, Henry. Tsui cannot understand what Henry is trying to say; that he has waited almost seven years to say it is even more confusing.

Madame Chu appears for the occasion dressed like a vision out of the early Qing dynasty. She wears a yellow kesi dragon robe, worked with gold dragons amid flaming pearls, with bats, fish, clouds and chrysanthemums floating above foaming and rolling waves. Around her neck she wears a necklace of Buddhist prayer beads, numbering 108 and made from perfectly matched pearl-sized white jade.

Madame Chu is widely known throughout the Chinese community in San Francisco for her remarkable ability to contact spirits of the dead. She never charges money for her service, but always receives generous offerings from her clients. Today, Madame Chu senses that she will be well compensated for her time; for several years Tsui had been "jing yi," a struggling woman in humble circumstances, but there have been recent changes in her home that smell of new money, of fresh-cut flowers and rare sandalwood incense.

Madame Chu's face mirrors Tsui's confusion. She cannot understand why Tsui cannot hear the spirit's message, for he is clearly standing beside her and shouting loudly in her ear. It doesn't require Madame Chu's extraordinary sensitivity to contact this spirit; one would have to be deaf and blind to avoid him. All Tsui hears is a ringing in her ears; all she sees is a wind chime stir in air that is perfectly still.

The spirit of the young man turns to Madame Chu and introduces himself, and Madame Chu understands the source of Tsui's confusion: the spirit bumping around Tsui's house is not her husband, Henry, but the shade of Keui-Sen Tung, Henry's murderer.

Tsui watches intently as Madame Chu appears to drift into a trance, but the elegant old woman is transfixed by Tung's story. "I am not dead," Tung explains. "I am laying in a hospital bed two thousand miles away. The mind is unconscious, and I was free to move about at will until I came to this place."

Madame Chu turns her attention to Tsui, and tries to explain Tung's dilemma, like an overseas operator trying to patch a bad connection. Tsui cannot understand how the living can leave a ghost; that it is her husband's murderer gives her the creeps.

"What we know of life is so much less than what there is to know," says Madame Chu, "except that there is no end. Tung is in transition between this world and the next."

Tsui is adamant. "Tell him to stop wandering around and go back to his own body," she tells Madame Chu.

"He doesn't want to go," Madame Chu responds. "He says that these affairs are part of one big plot. Even if he goes back to his body there are people waiting to kill him."

Tsui searches her living room for some sign of Tung. She shivers at the thought that she is living with his ghost; it is immoral, it's like cheating on her husband.

"Tell him I forgive him," Tsui says.

"He knows," says Madame Chu. "He is being very gracious. He wants to speak to his wife and sister."

"Then he should go to their house," Tsui suggests.

Madame Chu listens intently to Tung's description of his torment. "I am stuck here," Tung tells her. "This is where I committed the worst crime. I can't leave."

Again, Madame Chu attempts to explain Tung's predicament to Tsui, who is unwilling to accept these conditions. "There is only one thing to do—" says Madame Chu.

"Move," Tsui interjects.

"…Bring his wife and sister for him to talk to."

"Here?"

"Here, to settle these affairs," says Madame Chu. "To bring rest to a lost soul."

# Chapter One:

## *Old Duck*

15 October 1984

Eight o'clock in the morning, and the Liu household is in an unusual uproar. Henry watches bemused as his wife, Tsui, hurries their two children out the door of their modest home in Daly City, and into the car. Most days the morning ritual goes off without a hitch in a smooth and orderly fashion; today is total chaos, they're late for school. Today is different. Today is not the same.

In her haste, Tsui notices two young Chinese men pass by on bicycles. She thinks she recognizes them, but they have baseball caps pulled low over their faces. She has seen them around the neighborhood before so she pays them little attention, although a hint of suspicion crosses her mind.

The cyclists are named Wu Duen and Kuei-Sen Tung. They have traveled a long distance on special assignment, and on this beautiful fall morning have found the man they are looking for at home. They circle the block, disappearing from Tsui's view, hide their bikes in the underbrush and scale a fence designed to prevent motorists from going over a Cliff. Hiding among the rocks, Wu and Tung keep a watchful eye on the Liu house.

Unbeknown to the Lius, Wu and Tung have made a practice of spying on their home during the past few days. They monitor the family's comings and goings, and have the Liu's schedule down pat; they know Tsui is late getting the kids off to school, know too, that it will take twenty minutes for her return. And they know that sometime during her absence, Henry will be leaving for his pottery shop located near Fisherman's Wharf. Wu and Tung decide to proceed with their plan.

Circling the block once more on bikes, Wu and Tung find the door to the Liu's garage open and Henry's car inside. This is their chance. They put down their bikes on the lawn in front of the neighbor's house and slip into the Liu's garage unnoticed. The garage is packed with shipping boxes from Taiwan and Hong Kong marked "Fragile," stacked so high as to block the light from the windows. There is barely enough room to park Tsui's Honda and Henry's Datsun.

In the darkness of the garage, Wu and Tung cannot see clearly. Wu hides beside the driver's side of the Datsun while Tung squeezes between the passenger side and a wall of boxes. The morning air is heavy, hearts pump from exertion, and it takes great effort to breathe. The pressure around them is like the abyss of an ocean. Drops of sweat dot the concrete surface where they crouch waiting, but neither man makes a move to wipe his face. Overhead are sounds of approaching footsteps, the two men frozen to their spot in anticipation.

Suddenly there are footsteps on the stairs leading from the kitchen to the garage. Tung rises up and sees a shadow but not a face.

"Is that him?" Tung whispers to Wu.

Their eyes meet, but Wu makes no answer.

Wu and Tung pull pistols from beneath their sweat suits. As a man comes around the left side of the car, Wu springs to his feet. "Henry! You fuckin' idiot! Think there is no one in the States to teach you a lesson? Kneel down!"

But Henry does not obey. Instead of kneeling, he lunges forward and grabs Wu by the throat, squeezing in an effort to shatter his windpipe. As they struggle, Wu fires a shot point blank into Henry's head, the bullet entering the right side of his nose and striking the left side of his brain. Henry releases his grip on Wu, and then loses his balance. He falls against his car and slides to the floor.

Tung has not moved a muscle during the fight. He is paralyzed with fear. He had come a long way on this mission, and here Wu has done all the dirty work. He is losing face in front of his partner. Tung stares into Henry's face to make sure they have the right man, sees that his lungs still draw life, then fires a bullet into Henry's stomach and a second shot into his chest. And for good measure-just to show his partner that he hasn't lost his nerve—Tung sends a third slug into Henry's heart. Now Tung and Wu are even.

Stuffing their pistols into the waistband of their sweatpants, the assassins hurry from the garage. As they ride away on their bikes, they are surprised that four gunshots seem not to have disturbed the neighbors. Slowing down to avoid suspicion from passersby, they approach a van waiting for them a few blocks away.

Wu drops his bike at the curb and jumps into the van. In a panic, Tung tries to stuff his bike through the van's hatch.

"Forget it!" Wu shouts. "Get in!"

Tung drops his bike and runs to catch the van as it pulls away from the curb, and within moments they disappear into the stream of the morning rush hour.

While in transit, Wu and Tung shed their sweat suits and wigs and stuff them into a sack that is ditched before they reach their destination. Arriving at a supermarket parking lot, they find their contacts, Little Pee and Little Yu, waiting for them. One look at Wu and Tung and they don't have to ask if the mission has been accomplished.

The plan now calls for the assassins to split up and meet again later: Tung goes with Little Pee and Little Yu, leaving Wu and the getaway driver to dispose of the rental van. Little Yu drives off with no sense for where he's headed, and spends the next two hours trying to find Chinatown-what is normally for him a short ride that he knows like the bottom of his favorite teacup.

Back at the Liu house, Henry's widow has just returned from her morning errand to find her husband dead in a pool of blood and grease, his eyes wide open as if he had not wanted to leave this world.


At the secret meeting place later in the evening of this same day, the gang assembles at the designated hour of eight o'clock. Twelve hours had elapsed since the murder of Henry Liu, but the participants in the plot are still edgy as news bulletins fill the airwaves.

"You've been hiding the truth!" Little Yu screams at an old man who sat at the head of a long table.

"Quiet, cockroach!" Tung admonishes him. "No one speaks to Old Duck in this manner!"

Little Yu sulks in a corner, with Little Pee's arm around his shoulder.

Wu Duen enters, nods to Tung, and then bows to Old Duck.

The old man smiles at Wu. "Congratulations on a job well done. Today you have eliminated an evil traitor to the mother country. You have provided a valuable service to your nation, and such actions are reasonable in the presence of urgency." Turning his gaze upon Little Pee and Little Yu, Old Duck adds, "Some of us, however, appear to be in great distress. You are tired, that is understandable. So, our meeting is cancelled. We meet tomorrow, same time, at Eastern Jade Villa."

With praise from Old Duck, a sense of relief filters through the room. The gang members move off in search of something to numb their highly agitated senses.

"Make sure they return home safely tonight," Old Duck says to a lackey, and with an obedient nod, the foot soldier disappears hot on the heels of the gang members.

Old Duck is alone now. Picking up a telephone receiver, he pushes a button on a tape recorder patched into the telephone line and places a call to Taiwan. He asks to be connected to Deputy Director Chen Hou-Men of the Information Agency, and when the call is forwarded to Chen, Old Duck gives the password: "The contract has been signed."

"Who are our partners?" Chen asks.

"Wu Duen and Kuei-Sen Tung."

"I will advise Director Wang," Chen says. "Return to Taiwan. Bring the partners with you. Bring copies of local newspapers."

Old Duck pauses. Returning to Taiwan immediately is a reasonable request, but why would the Agency want him to bring Wu and Tung with him? This is unusual.

Chen senses Old Duck's suspicion. "We must control information revealed. We do not want our partners discussing our business. Better if they are here at home than there, where loose talk would be highly dangerous. Here, they will be received like heroes. There, they must be silent as the grave."

"I will bring them home," Old Duck says, reluctantly. Returning the receiver to its cradle, he rewinds the tape and plays it back until dawn.


16 October 1984


Old Duck gathers his gang at Eastern Jade Villa. The restaurant is owned by Koreans who do not know the identity of Old Duck and his followers, except to know that it is better for them if they don't know. For everywhere in Chinatown, this party of eight was instantly recognized as members of the notorious Tsu-Len Gang.

Tsu-Len Gang was a widely known and dreadfully feared organization that had been terrorizing Taipei for thirty years. Originated in 1961 by college students who went about imitating real gangsters, they drank blood during initiation rites, swore oaths of allegiance and instituted a system of passwords and mystics. Leave it to some misguided youths to take this nonsense seriously; out of charades and youthful hijinks, a far more deadly game grew.

Within five years of its inception, Tsu-Len Gang grew into five branches-or generations-symbolized by the Lion, Tiger, Leopard, Phoenix and Duck. And with the dissolution of the ruling gang, Tsu-Len ruled Taipei. By 1965, Tsu-Len Gang peaked as the largest gang in the world, swallowing up smaller gangs in the province. After unifying the gangs of Taipei, Tsu-Len merged with other prominent gangs throughout the rest of the world. Their numbers were greater than any other international organization, legitimate or otherwise.

As a tribute to the invisible kingdom of Tsu-Len, one of the more literate members wrote a poem that became an anthem for their movement:

> Bamboo leaves move and grow
> Sands blow,
> Within thousands of miles in the Tsu-Len grove
> Standing tall,
> Above all,
> Bamboo arrogantly smiles at itself.

And the man who stood alone at the top of Tsu-Len Gang, smiling arrogantly at himself, was none other than Old Duck, Chen Chi-Li.


On the evening of 16 October, Old Duck sits at the head of a large round table-the head, according to Chinese custom, being the one who faces the door—as waiters trundle platters of Eastern Jade Villa delicacies from the steamy kitchen. The food is placed on a lazy susan in the center of the table, and everyone waits for Old Duck to sample each offering first. The table fairly groans under the weight of the repast. In place of a floral centerpiece, a stack of San Francisco newspapers-American and Chinese-is piled on the table. Details of the Liu murder are shouted from every headline.

Old Duck spears a succulent dumpling with a chopstick, surveys the banquet for his favorite flavors, and notices that his entourage appears to have lost their appetite; they take small helpings and pick at grains of rice with intense interest. All except for Wu Duen, who looks as though he hasn't eaten in weeks. He shovels mouthfuls of noodles into his face, unconcerned by the discomfort of his mates.

"How can you eat like this, with all that staring you in your face?" Little Pee challenges Wu Duen.

"If the news upsets you, little brother, perhaps you shouldn't read the paper," Wu replies, between mouthfuls.

"But it's in all the papers," Little Pee cries. "There's no escaping it. This man was important…"

"So?"

"This man is known in Washington…

"So?"

"This man," Little Pee says pointedly, "was *American* citizen. He is known."

Wu Duen puts down his bowl and picks up a newspaper from the stack. "Let's see what is known," Wu says, and then highlights the first clues to emerge from the investigation. "Police say no valuables taken, so, no robbery. Police say no secret love affair, so, no jealousy. That leaves business—"

"Or politics," says Tung.

Wu Duen continues to read. "FBI involved. There is checkpoint at LAX… all Asians are being questioned."

This item draws the first noticeable reaction from Old Duck. "We are to return home tomorrow," he states. "How long will this interrogation of passengers go on?"

"Two men were seen in Liu's neighborhood for many days," Wu reads, without answering Old Duck's question. "The police have drawing of the suspects, but they look like…

"Who?" Tung interjects nervously.

" Mexicans," Wu smiles.

Old Duck clears his throat to speak. "Victim is Chinese, suspect is Chinese. Our trip home is postponed."

"Now what?" Little Pee wants to know.

"Now," Old Duck says, "We finish our dinner."

After dinner, Old Duck returns to a safe house bringing his gang with him. He doesn't want them running loose, with police and FBI about, and he wants to allay their fears lest panic cause them to accidentally expose themselves. Gathering the boys around him, he speaks in a low, confident tone.

"What are you afraid of?" Old Duck asks.

There is no reply, only blank expressions.

"If you do not know what you are afraid of, then you are afraid of nothing. And there is nothing for my friends to fear. I will tell you a secret: I am an Information Agent. I have many good relationships with powerful government officials at home. I know I will not have any trouble, but I also know each of you worries for himself. It seems there may be much more to our unfortunate victim than even I was made aware. And there is the chance that all of us, including myself, could be arrested after we return to Taiwan."

The boys are transfixed, searching Old Duck's face for meaning, then looking at one another for support. Old Duck reaches into his coat pocket and retrieves two cassette tapes, placing them on the table.

"Our only guarantee is these two tapes," Old Duck says. "If we are arrested, copies of these tapes will be made public."

The boys stare at the tapes and wonder what message is so powerful that it could spring them from jail.

"I am not worried," Old Duck reassures them. "You guys are my good brothers. I won't allow anything to happen to you."

Had this promise been made by anyone else, chances are it would not have held much meaning for these boys. But this is Chen Chi-Li. This is the boss of Tsu-Len Gang. Only he could make such promises.

The boys take some comfort from Old Duck's words; they have no other source of relief. And yet, interest in the murder of Henry Liu was continuing to receive increasing attention. The State of California was asking the federal government to take over the investigation. Just who was this Henry Liu?


18 October 1984

Old Duck moves his gang to Los Angeles by car. They are able to contact a Tsu-Len Gang member named Yellow Bird, who is to solve the dilemma of how to spirit the killers out of the U.S. and back to Taiwan. Yellow Bird has seen federal agents swarming LAX, and he deems it too risky to pass through customs. He suggests Old Duck and the boys fly to Houston, and then take a flight home via Dallas. Yellow Bird has a business front in Houston; they will be safe with him.

At Yellow Bird's house in Houston, a constant barrage of telephone calls come from Taiwan, demanding Old Duck return with Wu and Tung immediately. Old Duck suggests that they take an alternate route, through Mexico or Canada, to avoid raising suspicion by flying directly to Taiwan. But Deputy Director Chen of the Information Agency is insistent: leave from Dallas direct to Taipei, and do it now.

Old Duck has no choice but to relocate to Dallas, and wait for Yellow Bird to arrange the tickets. Passage for Old Duck, Wu Duen and Kuei-Sen Tung is booked for 21 October. Before he boards the plane, Old Duck meets with one of his closest stateside allies, An-Le Chang, aka White Wolf. Their exchange is brief, and as they shake hands Old Duck slips White Wolf a small package containing two cassette tapes.

"Keep these in a safe place," Old Duck says. "If anything happens to me, you will be contacted and told what to do with them."

On the way to Dallas airport, Kuei-Sen Tung has ominous feelings of dread. He isn't sure he wants to go, and run the risk of being stopped at customs. But he has faith in his leader. "Old Brother, you decide," Tung says to Old Duck. "If something goes wrong, I am willing to take all responsibility for the murder, as long as I have your promise to take care of my family."

Old Duck is moved by Tung's loyalty. He cannot speak, but nods in agreement. He thinks of the mission, of the Agency, and of the odd request to return home with the partners. All of it made Old Duck uneasy, but the order came from on high.

The trio splits up at the terminal. Old Duck enters first, then Wu and Tung by separate entrances. They are instructed to run in the event Old Duck is stopped by police. Unexpectedly, everything goes smoothly; they hop a flight to Japan, and transfer to Taipei.

Escaping the United States was but half of the ordeal. What awaited them at home? Is their return a celebration or a trap?

The plane lands at nine p.m. Old Duck, Wu and Tung exit together and find Deputy Director Chen Huo-Men waiting for them at the gate, surrounded by security. They are briefly greeted, then rushed through a gate marked "Official Use Only," and pass through customs without stopping. A black sedan idles curbside in front of the terminal, in the middle of a military motorcade. They are quickly ushered inside, and the motorcade speeds away from the terminal and through police checkpoints without stopping.

Their destination is one of the nicest restaurants in Taipei, where they are treated to a sumptuous feast. And then Deputy Director Chen speaks for the first time that evening. "The boss is very happy with your contribution to the nation," he says. "And the big boss is very happy, too. This situation has been very difficult, and what we need most are men like you. In fact, we could use more men like you nice fellows, with pure thoughts devoted to our country."

The rest of Chen's speech is forgotten as he spills $40,000 in U.S. currency onto the table. "As a reward," Chen says, with a magnanimous sweep of his arms.

Wu and Tung sit motionless in stunned silence. Prepared for the possibility of being arrested, they find themselves praised and paid off in a grand manner. There was only one thing for cautious men to do: refuse.

"As citizens of Taiwan, we consider our contribution to be only the obligation of a citizen," Wu says, speaking for Tung as well. "We have no expectation of reward, and cannot accept this money."

Now it was Deputy Director Chen's turn to be surprised. If ever he had and ulterior motive, it vanished in the face of such patriotism, such loyalty. And so he lets the partners in on recent developments which they find helpful: "The State Department of the United States is making a formal inquiry here, and American agents are pressing their sources for leads. Therefore, you must seal your mouths completely-even to parents and wives, and you need not fear anything from the Agency. Word of this will reach the top, of your great deeds. Even if the police arrest you, you will not be sent to jail."

Strange feelings descend on Wu and Tung. "Only a few hours ago at the airport we were surrounded by police who treated us like diplomats," Tung says. "Why do we risk arrest by these same police? Can't the Agency hold them off?"

"We have informed the Attorney General," Chen says. "There won't be any problem. But as there are many locally born Taiwanese in various police units, some of them have connections outside the KMT. If the truth were spilled, I wouldn't know what to expect. After careful consideration, however, I want you to know that the Agency has not revealed your identities to police, even to those who are our friends."

Chen's words sound reasonable to Wu and Tung if for no other reason than it seems the plot had been carefully laid and all angles considered. Even if what Chen says isn't completely true, his assurances temporarily relieve the partners.

Chen continues to lavish praise on the partners during the remainder of the meal. "Perhaps you would be interested in joining the Agency," Chen ventures. "As I said before, we could use more courageous patriots like you."

Of course, the offer comes as another big surprise to Wu and Tung, since consideration for the Agency was the highest honor their country could bestow upon the low born; it was exulting to their ancestry. And as Deputy Director Chen outlines the training they would receive from the Agency, the reward money continues to sit on the table, seemingly forgotten. If Wu and Tung look at the loot they are careful not to stare, for Chen keeps his eyes locked on theirs, like a high stakes poker game.

But the glazed look from the partners, the thing that puts the gleam in their eyes is not cash, it is the hypnotizing prospect of becoming Information agents and working for the only organization in Taiwan with more power than Tsu-Len Gang.

There they sat, two assassins in a tug of war between two very powerful yet very different warlords-Deputy Director Chen Hou-Men of the Information Agency and "Old Duck" Chen Chi-Li of Tsu-Len Gang. At first glance, one would think they were polar opposites as leaders of the government's intelligence branch and the largest criminal enterprise in the world; that the two forces had come together for the sole purpose of eliminating Henry Liu caused Wu and Tung to wonder if the two entities were somehow one and the same. After all, Old Duck had previously revealed his identity as an Information agent.

And what did this bizarre set of circumstances say about Henry Liu, that it required this unique collaboration in order to erase the threat that he posed?

Like layers of an onion, the strange case of Henry Liu seemed to deepen by many fine layers-the deeper it went, the stranger it got. No one could be trusted, and the partnership between Wu and Tung seemed to be at odds sometime with the partnership of Chen and Old Duck: having already pledged their sworn blood oaths to one, how could they do the same for the other?

In a conflict between the Information Agency and Tsu-Len Gang, there was no question which side would win.

Or was there?

# Chapter Two

## *Henry*

1932

A time of great suffering fell upon our land. War between Jiang Jieshi's Kuomintang government and the Communist rebels led by Mao Zedong captured our people in the middle. Everywhere was confusion and instability; every man, woman and child cautiously sought a quiet corner in which to survive.

The villagers of Jing-Jiang—a rural area in the north of Jiang-Sue province—had always maintained a detached attitude towards politics; "The sky is high and the emperor far away," and so we rarely concerned ourselves with the workings of government. We were too busy trying to find food for our tables. But as the great chaos spread from the cities to the villages, the serenity of Jing-Jiang was shattered. Landlords of the community frightened us with ominous threats that Mao would seize our land and possessions, and so we banded together into a ragtag militia—the Bao-An-Tun—to protect our homes and families.

The Bao-An-Tun was an effective line of defense for rural areas such as Jing-Jiang, which was too far away from the cities for the Kuomintang to protect. Under the command of Jiang Liu, the farmers of our village became skilled guerillas, killing a great number of Communists. In December 1932, Jiang Liu's wife bore him a son, named Jiang Nang. The father raised the son in his image, with a love for our land and a hatred for the Communists who threatened our way of life.

Jiang Liu and Jiang Nang were constant companions. The education the child received from his father was superior to what he would learn later in school. What is more, father and son were best friends, rarely apart. "Liu and his shadow" is how we referred to the pair. And that is the loving way they remained for many years.


The winter of Jiang Nang's tenth birthday was brutally cold. He often was made to remain at home while his father went out alone on Bao-An-Tung business, a separation that made the boy uneasy as if the bond between them was being stretched out of all proportion. And then came the morning when Jiang Nang heard the unmistakable echo of two gunshots shortly following his father's departure. He ran out of the house to find his father lying motionless in the middle of the frozen dirt road. He was shot through the head. The ground around him was covered in blood. Jiang Nang wailed like a siren from the depths of his being; the scene so firmly etched in memory that there would never be any escape from its terror: the deep red blood of his father frozen on the crisp white snow, traces of which the cruel and unrelenting winter preserved for months; forever fresh in Jiang Nang's mind.

After his father's murder, the responsibility of disciplining Jiang Nang fell to his grandfather. The old man was very strict, molding his charge into the very best Chinese mythical dragon. For the next six years, Grandfather was tyrannical in his approach to the boy's education and forced him to study the wisdom of the sages, especially the "Gu Wen Guan Tsi," (The Collection of Ancient Articles). The Articles were difficult to comprehend, but provided Jiang Nang with the sound background in literature that would serve him throughout his life as a writer. Although

Grandfather was strict with him, Jiang was still a vivacious child. He was at home in the countryside; listening to the birds sing and watching the fish swim, nurturing his love and veneration for the freedom for which his father had given his life.

In 1948, the Kuomintang instituted a spate of political reforms. The golden yuan and silver yuan currencies were printed limitlessly, causing inflation to skyrocket, shattering China's economy. Shanghai fell under forced economic control that spread to the rural areas. Jiang's home, hundreds of miles away, did not escape. The local shops ran out of rice and Jiang's family scavenged for food. Setting out for the neighboring village of Gu-Shan, they found poverty one step ahead. The only source of relief came from the other side of the world: sacks of flour labeled in English, "USA."

Jiang graduated from junior high school that same year, and found his education suddenly at an end. In the six years following his father's murder, the Communists had overrun his village, forcing his family to seek refuge in the countryside. In August, another crop of reforms was implemented to provide economic relief. This new vision of bread to fill empty stomachs was what Jiang Nang's father had always referred to as "revealing only the best." He was wise to the reality and saw the desperation of the government's situation right away. This boy from the country understood the difficulty in staying put, the impossibility of returning home, and came to the inevitable conclusion to head south to the city.

Jiang Nang, along with his little brother, packed his few possessions and left their mother's home. On the road they met countless others heading in all directions, each bearing the same burden brought on by war. Starving, barely surviving, the brothers arrived at Soochow. There they found no alternative to joining the Kuomintang Army, sacrificing their farm-fresh freedom for the rigors of soldiery; anything for a hot meal and a warm place to sleep.

Jiang Nang barely tolerated life in the barracks. After a few months of enlistment—rested and fit—the idea of deserting the ranks crossed his mind. He planned with some newfound friends to run away, but as details of the escape formed, the Communists crossed the river in a full-scale assault of Soochow. The boys could either die fighting or die running; they figured they had a better chance remaining with the army.

The KMT troops withdrew from Soochow to Shanghai in the following year, dragging Jiang Nang and his brother in their wake. The world they had known had fallen apart, turning into a hell of battles. Like small boats on a stormy sea, Jiang Nang and his brother were set adrift among the gales that constantly threatened their survival.

As the elder brother, Jiang Nang was expected to look after his sibling, even though the weight of decision-making was too heavy for a 17-year-old to handle. In contemplating his fate, too often he considered options that wandered too close to the edge. He could not decide what was best for him while fearing for his brother's safety, and so Jiang Nang told his little brother to go back home to mother. As for himself, Jiang Nang decided to flee the mainland, and hopped a freighter to Taiwan.

Uncertainty loomed like Mount Meru: Jiang was approached on deck by a KMT senior officer whom he thought would have him cast in irons until a court martial and execution could be arranged. But the miracle of fortune was pleasing, and Jiang found a friend in the officer instead of a prosecutor. The voyage passed deep in conversations which lasted late into the night, and while they discussed all subjects—from personal heroes to political problems—the officer never got around to questioning Jiang's purpose.

As the freighter docked in Taiwan, the officer insisted that Jiang accompany him to KMT Army headquarters. Fearing at the last minute he had fallen into a trap, Jiang was led into the commander's office and—without ceremony or fanfare—was elevated to the rank of lieutenant by his friend. While trying to desert the ranks, Jiang had talked his way into becoming-at seventeen—the youngest military officer in the KMT Army.

At the KMT barracks in Taiwan, the troops were undergoing a reorganization that periodically disrupted the ranks like a Chinese fire drill. Soldiers packed, stacked and moved their gear about the compound in delirious maneuvers, only to return to their starting point. The captain leafed through his muster sheet with a quizzical look, wondering who in the world was Lt. Jiang Nang; there was no such person on file, he seemed to have been born from a rock.

"You are no longer Lieutenant," the captain said, sternly.

The boy stared back at the captain, fearing he had been exposed as an imposter.

"You are now First Lieutenant," the captain declared, and thrusting the muster sheet into the boy's trembling hands, turned on his heels and departed, never to be seen again.

For the next twelve months, Jiang wandered about from post to post, a lonely first lieutenant in search of a command that continued to elude him.


At the end of 1950, Jiang entered the Political Staff College managed by the ministry of Defense. His junior hi education was-in the opinion of this 18-year-old officer—keeping him from rising further in the ranks. The school was located in Shan-Chi in the Shin-Chu province. The headmaster was none other than "Prince" Jiang Jingguo, son of the president of Taiwan, who felt it was particularly inspiring to broadcast recordings of pep talks by his father to the students at all hours of the day and night. The speeches were tedious and endlessly boring, teeming with courage and confidence: "Prepare in one year, return in two years, fight in three years, and succeed in five years!" Many of his classmates were impressed, however Lt. Jiang was disgusted with the clichés of Jiang Jieshi, and his country bred common sense told him those slogans "revealed only the best." In his mind Jiang heard the voice of his father chide, "Return in two years?! Nonsense! For you, my son, there is no returning to Mainland China."

While at Political Staff College, Jiang veered far from military matters. He majored in Theatre, and held a job as entertainment reporter for the school newspaper. He also contributed biographical sketches to the Chen-Shen radio network programme, "Three Thousand Walks of Life." He had a nose for news, his Mandarin accent being the only element holding him back from becoming a major on-air personality.

At long last Jiang found the perfect path to lead him away from the military toward a more profitable, peaceful and fruitful life: communications. He came under the tutelage of Chen-Shen radio's general manager, Mr. Hsia, who took special interest in the cub reporter who now preferred to be called "Henry Liu" instead of Jiang Nang. A change in name underscored a general makeover: "Henry" shed Lt. Jiang's KMT Army tunic for a dark blue coat, rejecting the untidy and unkempt appearance that was the uniform and fashion of journalists of that time. The impression Henry gave Mr. Hsia was one of always being in a hurry.

When Henry spoke, Mr. Hsia held his breath and struggled to understand the rapid-fire cadence of declarations that went off like a string of firecrackers. And in that regard, Henry cut a stronger military image than Lt. Jiang.

So complete was the makeover that Lt. Jiang disappeared entirely. When KMT officials came to find him he was gone, leaving only a Mr. Henry Liu behind. Since he had held no particular command in the army, the KMT simply removed the name Jiang Nang from its muster and forgot he ever existed.

The last stroke in the portrait of the new man was the boldest: a new motorcycle, which represented the independence he had been seeking since the violent interruption of his childhood. But this independence—hard fought and long awaited did not last long. Henry became a new father to a son of his own.

## 1959

As Chen-Shen radio went about hurried preparations for the big journalism trade show and exhibition in Taipei, Mr. Hsia was suddenly inspired to invite Henry Liu's beautiful wife to join the work force, and as Liu-Min slipped into the new exhibition uniform—gray with white stripes—she looked so elegant that everyone's eyes fell on her.

The exhibition was widely known in Taipei, collecting journalists from every newspaper firm, small and large. Among the throng of reporters was an acquaintance of Henry's who ran an entertainment column in The Daily News whose name was Yao. Chen-Shen's booth especially attracted him. He came to the booth every day and stayed until closing. Even an insensitive person could see that Yao's intention was not on Chen-Shen but Liu-Min. All this newfound attention was not lost upon the girl. Perhaps it was weakness in her personality, perhaps it was weariness from slipping down Henry's list of priorities, but the direction light of the Liu marriage turned from cautionary yellow to red. They had been such an admirable, happy couple, but this unpredictable change brought about a disastrous conclusion.

Henry granted Liu-Min a divorce. After three years of marriage he got his freedom back, along with a little son. It mattered not, the break-up of his home, for Chen-Shen had become the largest radio network in Taiwan with fourteen stations in major markets, and as the fame of general manager Hsia spread, so did the name of Henry Liu, Hsia's understudy. Henry lived the good life, and feminine companionship was not a pressing problem.

Problems arose when Mr. Hsia got too big for his employers to control, and he was forced to resign. He used his estimable reputation to start up his own newspaper, The Taiwan Daily News. Rather than remain behind without his mentor, Henry jumped ship, too. Although Mr. Hsia had some initial doubts that Henry could make the transition—the job of a newspaper reporter is different from a radio station—Henry insisted on defecting to the TDN, winning over Mr. Hsia by agreeing to work on a probational basis and for a cut in pay.

It took Henry six months to polish his literary skills and perfect the art of the essay. His articles were characterized by a sharp criticism that showed no fear for anyone. He often showed his subjects no mercy. He published his comments under his given name, Jiang Nang, as if the makeover that had forced him into hiding from the army could now be washed away to reveal the true man: what emerged from his unmasking was anger over his father's murder which had been suppressed for too long. He went about his task with such vim and vigor that it created an odd polarity in his employer: Mr. Hsia admired Jiang's essays but necessarily suffered the recriminations of important politicians whose feelings were injured by Jiang's sharply pointed pen. Thus, the stage was set for tragedy.

Henry, as he was still called by friends, was turning thirty years old and once again came to a crossroad in his personal life. He met a girl named Tsui, who was a freshman at National Political University. Henry fell in love with Miss Tsui, but felt ashamed of himself, like a dying eagle. Miss Tsui, on the other hand, was blind to his detractions and with a vision so perfect went about secretly planning for their happiness. She provided him total encouragement and support, even when his employer didn't, and she went so far as to push Henry back into school and helped him learn English.

To Henry, learning English was like teaching an aborigine to ski. He had an extremely difficult time figuring out sentence structure, but with a fighting spirit he immersed himself into the world of English, except for eating and sleeping. He refused to listen to or read Chinese. He camped out all day at the U.S. Information Services, and made friends with every American he encountered, learning conversational English from them and teaching them Chinese in return. As a result of his dedicated effort, Henry passed his exams and at the same time obtained the undying love of Miss Tsui.

Dissatisfaction with his world increased in Henry. He needed space—not to move about as a boy in the country-but freedom for a wise man to develop into a wiser man. As great as China is, America was where he wanted to go. But America was difficult to reach without a guarantor to sponsor him, and no such person yet existed. And until a guarantor could be found, Henry continued to work at TDN by day and perfect his English at NNU by night.

Henry received many exciting responses from regular TDN readers who admired his sharp criticism of the Chinese political circus. Anger seethed from his pen, like blood dripping on crisp white newsprint; surprising how many angry people there are in this world. And so TDN became the voice of the angry and a paper of great importance, at the expense of Mr. Hsia's peace of mind, for with every Jiang Nang editorial there was the attendant complaint from its target. Perhaps it was a good idea, then, that Mr. Hsia assign Henry to Hong Kong for awhile, giving everyone a much needed break.

Henry's experiences in Hong Kong were enough to fill a book. At the end of his sabbatical he collected his essays into "The Trip to Hong Kong," which Mr. Hsia published. The book sold so well that Mr. Hsia dispatched Henry to manila, Saigon and other places of interest for the same purpose. The results were so favorable that Henry hatched a brilliant plan: he would go to America as TDN's correspondent, and Mr. Hsia would be his guarantor. The second act of Henry's life was now rolling up the curtain; the United States, heaven of freedom, opened her welcoming arms.


Patience. In a word, patience is what it means to be Buddhist, what it means to understand the Chinese mentality. Henry was fond of telling friends "Learning English and finding a way to

America was the most patient thing I've ever done." And the second most patient thing he did was to marry Miss Tsui after a five-year courtship, for he married not out of love or desire but out of a genuine sense of gratitude for her investment in his education. It was hard for him to explain why romance had vanished leaving only obligation in its place, but if Washington D.C. was Henry's prize, it was only right to share it with the woman who had worked so hard to help him win it.

Henry's arrival in Washington was like being born into a new life of intellectual freedom. He had never felt like this before, anywhere else in the world. Upon encountering the library at American University, he enrolled in the school of International Relations with the intention of reading every book he could lay hands on. Between classes, he found items of interest with which to patch together articles for TDN, and for which Mr. Hsia continued to send his meager wages.

Home. Henry's view of Taiwan was broader now that it was viewed through a telescope instead of a microscope. The vantage point from Washington was not like viewing flowers in the midst of Taiwan. Now he could see things more clearly, and the first person to emerge in a dramatic new light was Jiang Jingguo, who was picked to succeed his father Jiang Jieshi as president of Taiwan, and who had also been headmaster at Henry's alma mater. Jiang Jingguo was emerging as one of the most important Chinese politicians of this century, and was a subject of great interest to Henry's faculty advisor, Lord Michael Lindsay.

Lord Lindsay had left his family estate in England for China in 1937, to join the Sino-Japanese War. He taught at Yen-Ching University, and later married one of his Chinese students with whom he had two children. Now, thirty years on, Lord Lindsay taught Modern Chinese History at American University. He encouraged Henry to recall his experiences as a student of Jiang Jingguo and use it as a basis for a broader view of the man and politician. The only existing biography of Jiang was a brief account of his education in Russia. Lord Lindsay had every expectation that an up-to-date portrait would easily find a publisher.

Henry set about the task of compiling information for Jiang's biography by writing to mutual friends for their personal observations. Not surprisingly, most of his contacts failed to reply. There were two close associates, however, who provided a tremendous amount of background material, including insights into Jiang's thoughts, merits, contributions, and political ideology-true stories never before published-but provided to Henry only upon strictest conditions of anonymity.

Five years elapsed in the process of compiling the book, during which time Henry also completed his Master's degree. Tsui worked in order to support the family, which had grown in number, and Henry augmented his income from TDN by teaching Chinese. In 1972, Henry embarked upon a course of study for his doctorate, intent on becoming a professor, but more practical matters seemed to keep getting in his way.

At age 40, now the father of two children, Henry could no longer afford tuition. He applied for aide from the China International Foundation, an academic research organization, promising that the biography of Jiang Jingguo would be the result. A glowing letter of recommendation from Lord Lindsay accompanied the application, along with a letter from the Chinese ambassador to the United States. With such notable references, Henry was certain that funding from the foundation would come through.

Imagine Henry's surprise when the grant failed to appear. The rejection letter was polite, but stated no reason for refusal. But in a private telephone conversation with one of the foundation's Chinese directors, Henry was told in no uncertain terms that a book about Jiang Jingguo was sure to irritate the Taiwanese government, and that was to be avoided at all costs. As a result, Henry had no choice but to end both the book project and his doctoral studies.

Henry's anger with life's slings and arrows—so difficult for him to control-erupted again on the pages of The Taiwan Daily News. His articles, sharp as ever, continued to delight his fans while tormenting his targets. He had, for example, doggedly pursued the Chinese director of Foreign Affairs during his official state visit to Washington, and made disparaging remarks about the director's speeches, going so far as to make fun of his

Pidgin English. The director was so embarrassed by Henry's criticism that he compelled the Chinese embassy to file complaints at home with TDN.

Henry's vexation with the embassy could be traced to an earlier encounter: when applying to visit the U.S., the embassy took an unnecessarily long time to grant permission. Whenever Henry made inquiry, embassy officials seemed bothered. And so Henry could be counted on to vent his frustration through his newspaper column. He accused diplomats of skimming money from secret U.S. interests, thereby ruining the image of Chinese as corrupt. And as angry as Henry's comments made the embassy, the diplomatic corps were also that much afraid of Henry's further criticism. They were afraid to take him on while he was safe on American Soil; Henry knew it, and he didn't care.

Open minded and straightforward. That was America, and that was Henry; the two were meant for one another. America was Henry's paradise. His passion also allowed him to make friends easily. From students to businessmen, from scholars to important American government officials-everybody was Henry's friend, including a growing number of Chinese expatriates who shared his view of the political scene back home. There were too many friends to list, and their number continued to increase fast. Their support and encouragement comforted him most during times when fortune hid her face.

The biography of Jiang Jingguo, which Henry began in 1970 and suffered from lapses of inactivity, continued to haunt him. Word of its incubating existence had filtered throughout China, all the way to the top, and TDN readers were anxious to read whether Jiang Nang's treatment of the next president would be kind or characteristically caustic. Henry knew his readers wanted blood; knew, too, that his critics wanted neutrality, if he were to be fair. There could be no word of conjecture. And there could be no criticism based on Jiang's private life—that was absolutely essential, because in Chinese society such intrusion by the press is not condoned by any faction.

Henry had received warnings from some of his contacts that his biographical sketch should not be published. If it were well written, why, no one would care. But if it was classic Jiang Nang written with poison pen, then the book could harm others as well as the author himself. Even Mr. Hsia, his mentor and employer, made a special visit to Washington as a guest of the State Department in order to discourage Henry from his extra-curricular activity. It was unlikely that Henry would quit, though, and Mr. Hsia knew it before he boarded the plane.

"I have been working on this book a long time," Henry told Mr. Hsia. "It may be the only way I distinguish myself in this country. To ask me to abandon my goal is cruel, like asking a parachutist to throw away the parachute after jumping from the plane."

"That is alright for you to say while you sit comfy-cozy in America," said Mr. Hsia. "I must return to Taiwan where it is not so comfortable. I cannot afford to be associated with a book that paints an unflattering picture of the president. The paper cannot continue to print your articles. You must make a choice."

"I have a dream," said Henry. "I want to present my book about Jiang to the readers. I will be respected, and all concerned will realize a profit."

Mr. Hsia looked weary. At times such as these, his understudy had an exhausting effect. Their conversation lasted through the night, and the elder man could see he was losing ground with each passing hour. He made one final appeal to Henry: "I have always tried to be your friend," he said. "I have weathered many storms for you, attacks from those you have offended."

Henry smiled.

"I published you even when I knew you were wrong, even when I knew you to be dangerous," Hsia continued. "But this is a different matter. This is too dangerous. This time you may not know your attacker when you see him, for you may not know all those who you offend."

Mr. Hsia paused to allow the full force and effect of the threat to sink in. It sounded to Henry as if the words had been chosen for him and rehearsed several times. Mr. Hsia picked up a lacquer cup and saucer in the form of a peach, inlaid with mother-of-pearl, and stared at the green tea leaves as if he were trying to tell the future. He replaced the cup and saucer on the long, low table of tielemu wood and shifted his attention to a book on rare and important examples of Chinese calligraphy. Chinese have always placed the art of writing on the same level as painting, if not higher. Despite their personal content and ephemeral nature, the artistic quality of calligraphy is judged on the merit of the writing alone.

Mr. Hsia flipped through the pages of the book until he found Wang Xizhi's "Orchid Pavilion Preface (Lanting Xu)," recognizing the unique hand of the artist as well as discerning the personal style and source of technique. Carefully kept, the hand scroll had been precious to centuries of collectors. Mr. Hsia mentally retraced the path of the artist's brush, noting all the variations of tempo and shades of expression, the way in which the brush responded to the most subtle variations in pressure and ink flow-in effect, recreating the work with the twelfth century calligrapher in mind, as if he were Wang's editor.

Henry broke the silence. "I just can't quit," he said. "I must speak out."

"Then I cannot be responsible for what happens," said Mr. Hsia. "You will have to go forward without me, without TDN."

Mr. Hsia closed the book and set it aside. Rubbing his eyes as he always did at the end of a long day at the newspaper, he arose from his seat and took Henry's hand, perhaps for the last time.

"I hope you understand," Henry said, almost apologetically. "Especially you, my editor. You know my mind—"

"No," Mr. Hsia stopped him, "not any more. From this day forward, please, as your friend, do not say this. It will mean trouble for my family and me. I must go now."

Mr. Hsia wasted no time in making his exit. Once Henry had made up his mind it was useless to try to change it. Mr. Hsia hurried from Henry's home as if he were late for an important meeting, even though it was near dawn. "Good bye, Henry," he said. "Good luck."

As Mr. Hsia walked away, Henry felt a sense of loss unlike anything he had experienced since the death of his father. He returned to his study to contemplate his predicament. In his short lifetime he had journeyed from farm boy to soldier, deserter to officer, to journalist and grad student; from nothing to success, from impossibility to possibility, he acted well in any role and at the same time remained unsophisticated. Sufferings of life did not trouble him much for he always remained true to his nature.

He came to the logical conclusion that he must finish what he had started, even if it meant working without the financial safety net that Mr. Hsia provided. The writer who was always looking for renewal again crossed his personal boundary and stepped into a brave, new world with an adventurous spirit.

Henry signaled his new independence by moving from the suburbs to downtown Washington and opened a gift shop in a mall near the White House. Imported brass decorative items and handicrafts from Hong Kong and Taiwan—toys and trinkets, and the odd antique reproduction ginger jar and porcelain goldfish bowl. Taking advantage of American ignorance of all things Chinese, Henry boasted to little old ladies who came into his shop that such-and-such was the Empress Dowager's soup bowl, or such a pen once belonged to China's last emperor. His polished presentation of these instant heirlooms had customers reaching for their checkbooks, convinced that Henry had no idea of their real value. And who was going to tell them different?

At the end of a shop keep's day, Henry retreated to his home and work resumed on his pet project. He approached the biography of Jiang Jingguo with renewed energy, without support from foundations or academic organizations. He revised his drafts over and over so that his work not only read well but looked pretty on the page, in the tradition of the ancient calligrapher. His closest friends were paid the high compliment of receiving a copy of the manuscript for their review, and all of the critiques were highly complimentary.

The four chapters comprising his book were published by installments in a monthly magazine "Nan Pei Chi (The Pole of North and South)," in Hong Kong. Henry generally received favorable reviews, but a long list of adversaries who had been skewered in his newspaper column compelled critiques pointing out inaccuracies and errata. It was a book many a politician loved to hate; Henry's fans loved him even more.

On April 4, 1975, Jiang Jieshi passed away in Taiwan. His son succeeded him as president. Seizing the moment, the editor of Nan Pei Chi published Henry's biography in book form without his consent and replaced Henry's name on the cover with "Ding-Yea." By the time Henry discovered the release of his book, thousands of copies had been sold. He dashed off a hot letter to the editor and demanded and explanation and was told curtly, "Time is tight. If we don't print it, others will. As far as the name change," the editor added, "that was done for your own protection."

The unauthorized rush release of Henry's book belied the fact that it had taken the author years to research his subject. It had the appearance of an unofficial history—of value as a reference perhaps—but too loose in style. It appeared to some that Henry blurred the line separating criticism from blame, and crossed over the privacy fence too often for Chinese society. The book exposed Henry's own prejudice; he couldn't keep to the neutral middle ground, tending only to one side. As professor Wu Bing-Chung said in his review, "This is a book waiting for modifications."

In the three years following its release, the book earned a pot of money for its publisher in China, much less for its author in America. The instant heirlooms with which Henry flooded the Washington market were being exposed as fakes, and imperial tea sets were being unloaded at drastically reduced prices. In 1978, Henry moved with his family to San Francisco. They bought a house in Daly City, and opened a pottery shop near Fisherman's Wharf called La Figurine. Henry continued to import porcelain of mediocre quality claiming it was first quality, and salted the mine with a few genuine rarities to make the junk look better and to prove the self-proclaimed experts in oriental art. Most buyers couldn't tell the difference; snuff bottles, vases and bowls were ingeniously faked. In China, they were considered "copies"; they became "fakes" when they reached the West and sold as old and genuine. Copies melded into collections and with the passage of time became indistinguishable. Either way, customers paid extortionate prices, but Henry was so charming that many of them frequently dropped by just for a visit, to hear him rhapsodize on the rare pair of Fa Hua porcelain vases from the Ming dynasty, the painted gray pottery horse recently excavated from a royal tomb, or the Tang dynasty camel figurine-all of which had been made only a few days earlier.

Henry prospered in California. His anger with life subsided, and as he approached middle age even his writing took on a mellower tone. He was a prankster and a tease. When he spied a pretty face strolling along the wharf, he would point to his friend and say, "Hello, lady! My friend says you are very pretty, and would like to ask you out for a meal!" And whenever he chanced upon a busy restaurant, he would turn the "Closed" sign on the door, "to spread business to others." Henry was sometimes a man who was a child at heart.


President Nixon's visit to China in 1972 had opened a door in the iron gate. People around the world developed a curiosity for the country that had been largely inaccessible to foreigners. Even Chinese living abroad became nostalgic for their homeland that was experiencing a renaissance. Henry Liu was no exception. He had been gone more than thirty years, and he longed to see his family. He wanted to walk the fields of his youth and see for himself how his homeland had changed.

Henry's financial situation would not easily permit him a lengthy leave from La Figurine. The best way to return home would be to receive an invitation from Chinese authorities that would pick up the tab, and the best person to make such arrangements was an old friend in Washington named Long-Shi.

Long-Shi was the son of Long-Yun, "The King of Yunnan." Long-Yun had been a close associate of Mao Zedong, and there were many who speculated that Mao's victory over the Kuomintang had much to do with a significant role played by Long-Yun; they were good pals. And with this strong background, Long-Shi could come and go to China freely.

Long-Shi opened a Chinese restaurant in Washington D.C. catering to high-ranking government officials. Whenever Chinese diplomats visited the capitol, they would dine with Long-Shi. The importance of his establishment put Long-Shi in the highly prized role of middleman between Chinese and American businessmen. He was a translator, agent and promoter of interests flowing in and out of China. All of which gave Henry Liu a brilliant idea: he planned to write a biography of Long-Yun, and expected that the son would do everything in his power to help the author honor the father.

As expected, Long-Shi took care of all the arrangements and Henry was invited to make a triumphant return to China in November 1980. There were odd restrictions, however, which would not permit him to return to Jing-Jiang but would enable him to reunite with his family nearby. Henry was confused, and upon seeing his brothers and sister he felt uneasiness beneath their tears of joy. Their conversation did not flow from the heart, seemed strange and guarded.

Finally, Henry and his brother were able to take a stroll through the park away from Henry's escort, the peeking, and the bugging device. At last, the truth emerged about the suffering the family had gone through during the Revolution. And as sad as the revelations made Henry, he knew he could never write about it. "If I criticize the government of China," he later told his wife, "it would contradict their hospitality. If I praise them, it would contradict my own conscience."

In return for maintaining his silence, Henry was able to bring his brother to the United States for a lengthy visit. After two years, he returned home to Jing-Jiang a "rich man of ten thousand dollars," which was Henry's only consolation for having compromised his journalistic integrity.

In 1983, Henry was approached by the publisher of "The California Tribune" Chinese-American newspaper to publish his biography of Jiang Jingguo in the United States. Eight years had passed since the book had been published in Hong Kong under the pen name "Ding-Yea." Jiang was now president of ROC Taiwan, and many strides had been made to improve the quality of life there.

But Henry's attitude toward his work had changed. Like many writers, he wanted to take a fresh look at his subject, correct mistakes, and temper his tone. He wanted to delve further into Jiang's family background, the revolution in Jia-Hsin, the impact of Wu Kuo-Chen and Sun Yixian, and most particularly the conflict between Jiang and Ch'eng Ch'eng. As long as the subject is alive, Henry reasoned, his biography is incomplete.

Confronted with the book in its original form, Henry recognized the failure of his objectivity and that he was not likely to overcome it. He had always been known for his sharp criticism, and that hadn't changed. As rumors of the book's revival spread through Taiwan, newspapers and magazines showed interest in acquiring the copyright. When they also requested the "right to modify," Henry understood that they were merely fronting for the government. When this ploy failed, Taiwanese government officials contacted Henry directly and offered him money to abandon his project.

The offer of bribes fostered the old obstinacy in Henry. He was a self-sufficient American citizen, and he no longer felt beholden to Taiwanese authority. And so the government in Taiwan took another approach: they put the screws to Henry's publisher at "The California Tribune." Even though The Tribune was an American enterprise, the KMT overcame the distance by leaning on The Tribune publisher's father who lived in Taipei.

This approach failed, too. The Tribune was a corporation organized by ten principal shareholders, each an educated person with an interest in preserving history. Each had one vote; one shareholder could not alter the decision of the majority, and the decision to publish Henry's biography of Jiang passed six to four, protests from the KMT notwithstanding.

In the opinion of the Taiwanese government, the issue was still not settled. The case was taken up by the Information Agency, a shadowy organization that controlled censorship, and was assigned to Vice Director I-Ming Hu, who was ordered to stop publication of Henry's book, period. Hu thoroughly reviewed the KMT file on Henry Liu, aka Jiang Nang, and found perhaps the only person in Taiwan that Henry might listen to: his old friend and mentor, Mr. Hsia.

In the ten plus years since his last meeting with Henry in San Francisco, Mr. Hsia had not corresponded with his former understudy. And Mr. Hsia carefully explained that fact to Vice Director Hu, more for his own protection than Henry's. Mr. Hsia went so far as to refuse intervention on the Information Agency's behalf, claiming he no longer held sway over his ex-employee. But vice Director Hu would not take "no" for an answer.

"You and your wife have not seen your children in America for some time," Hu reminded Hsia. Hu had obviously done his homework, and at the mere mention of his children, Hsia's anxiety heightened. "I believe your son is studying at Berkeley, and your daughter is preparing for her doctorate at Harvard. I know they will be very happy to see their honorable parents."

Vice Director Hu dropped an envelope on the table containing three round-trip airfares to San Francisco—the extra ticket for Hsia's granddaughter—and two thousand dollars in U.S. currency. He said nothing more, leaving Hsia dumbfounded.

When Hsia landed in San Francisco with his wife and granddaughter, he was welcomed at the gate by his daughter-in-law and Henry Liu. They were whisked away to a marvelous dinner hosted by Henry, where conversation centered on culture and scenery and every other topic save publishing. Henry knew Mr. Hsia had something important to say but did not know where or how to start, so he ended his mentor's misery by declaring, "The publication of the book ceased the moment you stepped on this soil. All this I have done for you, my trusted friend."

Mr. Hsia should have had the sweetest sleep that night at his son's house.

After several days in Berkeley, Mr. Hsia went to Boston to visit his daughter. He spent a week there, then returned to San Francisco for the New Year. Mr. Hsia was invited to Henry's house for a party. There was plenty of good food and a full bar, and after several drinks that he was unaccustomed to having, Henry became quite talkative. And Mr. Hsia took advantage of the moment to bring up the touchy subject of the biography.

What Henry said came as quite a surprise to Hsia. "I recognize the great contributions made by Jiang in the past twenty years, especially after he became president. I suppose if I were to write the book today, I would tone it down with nicer words."

Mr. Hsia smiled and was visibly relieved.

Henry finished his drink. "Unfortunately, the printing plates have already been made, and the cost of Chinese plates in America is very expensive. "Henry laughed, as if he had made a funny joke.

Mr. Hsia did not join in the laughter. "How expensive?" he pressed.

"Oh, eight thousand dollars," he replied, and laughed uproariously as if it were the answer to a clever riddle.

"I do not have such a sum," Mr. Hsia said. "But perhaps I can arrange it when I return to Taiwan."

All traces of levity evaporated. "If you are speaking about the Information Agency, you are wasting your time," Henry said, deadly earnest, surprising his mentor with an uncanny ability to deduce the true purpose of Hsia's trip.

Taking Mr. Hsia by the arm, Henry led him further away from the party. "The director of the Information Agency is Hsi-Lin Wang," Henry said, his voice barely above a whisper. "While I was in Washington, Wang did many awful things there which I found out about and wrote on extensively. I did it to put him down. It was very effective."

Mr. Hsia knew what Henry meant; he need not elaborate on the details. And from the look on Henry's face, Hsia saw that there had been the kind of fallout from Wang that Hsia had faced on numerous occasions from the targets of Henry's articles.

"So," Henry said, pouring another drink, "I doubt there is much hope for the eight thousand dollars."

Mr. Hsia wasted no time in returning to Taiwan to advise Vice Director Hu at the Information Agency that Henry's biography of President Jiang was set to roll in its original unexpurgated form. He expressed his deep personal regret at his inability to intervene in this matter on the Agency's behalf, and Vice Director Hu forwarded the news to Director Hsi-Lin Wang. The next day, Director Wang called Hsia and said, "Okay, I will pay the eight thousand, but Henry Liu better keep his promises."


Henry received the money by wire transfer two days later. Mr. Hsia passed along the coded message from Chief Wang: "If you ever kept a promise, make certain you keep this one."

As promised, Henry modified the new edition of Jiang's biography to a kinder inclination. He lavished praise upon his contributions, and put a more positive spin on his criticisms. The modifications were obvious to readers of both versions, and the book was warmly received at home in Taiwan. The long-standing matter of rendering a finished product everyone could live with was finally resolved. Mr. Hsia quietly returned to his affairs, the Information Agency pursued other matters, and Henry Liu looked for new dragons to slay.

## 1984

Always searching for a story, Henry went across the United States twice to interview an 80-year-old Chinese immigrant in Georgia named Wu Kuo-Chen. The people of Savannah merely regarded him as a kindly old man who liked to view the ocean from Tybee Island, but the Chinese community recognized him as a former associate of Jiang Jingguo who had to flee Taiwan for his safety.

Old Wu had a wonderful story to tell, and Henry wanted to be the writer to tell it. Old Wu had also brought out of Taiwan all of his files intact, and therein lay a fascinating tale of intrigue, state secrets and locations of where all the bodies were hidden. What is more, Old Wu represented the enlightened attitude of so many Chinese Americans who embraced democracy and eschewed communism. And if President Jiang wanted old Wu dead, Henry wanted him—at age 80—very much alive.

Henry was onto the kind of story that wins Pulitzer prizes. He ventured back to Mainland China to collect information on Wu, using the old project about Long-Yun as his excuse so as not to arouse suspicions. Henry was received in China as a famous scholar and historian; his criticism of Taiwan's president was looked upon favorably, and there were many new friends who wished to be of every kind of assistance.

The most remarkable event came about when Henry was suddenly invited to return to the place of his birth, Jing-Jiang. Now 52 years old, he could scarcely remember what the village had looked like. He was surprised to receive a passionate welcome from local officials, and even more surprised to find that these were the same men who had murdered his father.

Face to face with the most defining moment of his life, Henry felt neither hatred nor revenge. He had come to terms with the war between the Kuomintang and the Communists long ago, and understood the political circumstances that had wreaked havoc on its civilian victims. Instead of anger, Henry was filled with curiosity and forgiveness towards his father's assassins, and spoke to them at length as if he were setting out on a new book venture-or putting the final touches on a story left unfinished too long.

Henry returned home to America a profoundly changed man. He volunteered to assist immigrants at the Chinese consulate in San Francisco. He held seminars on democracy and American politics for Chinese-Americans, and tutored their children in History, Economics, Geography, and Western Culture. He was putting the finishing touches on his biography of Old Wu, and had nearly completed his book about Long-Yun. He was productive as only a writer who is truly inspired can be, and a valuable asset to his community. Most of all, Henry was at peace with the world.

On 15 October 1984, Henry Liu was murdered.

# Chapter Three

## Old Duck

13 November 1984

Taiwanese newspapers shouted "Project Clean-Up!" Overnight, the Information Agency had cracked down on the notorious Tsu-Len Gang and arrested their leader, Chen Chi-Li, aka "Old Duck," Wu Duen, the gang's chief executioner, and three unnamed lackeys.

Three days later, on the 16th, "Thunder Weekly" published tips that Tsu-Len Gang was responsible for the murder of renowned journalist Henry Liu.

In Hong Kong, Wen-Hui News reported details of a tape recording sent to them from America, in which the Liu murder was spelled out step by step by Tsu-Len ganglord Old Duck. Simultaneously, CNN broadcast to Americans the findings that Old Duck and others had confessed the involvement of Taiwan's Information Agency in the murder.

The day after the news broke in Hong Kong and New York, AFF in Taipei telexed: "The Ministry of Defense of Taiwan announced that the head of the Information Agency has been temporarily suspended pending an investigation into the murder of Henry Liu.

And now, citizens of Taiwan and America came to realize the truth behind Henry's assassination: the veil had been lifted to reveal the death penalty for scholarship. What the world had yet to learn was why the Tsu-Len Gang executed a ChineseAmerican writer, and what was the connection between the gang and Taiwan's Information Agency.


Taiwanese journalists who considered themselves to be kindred spirits to Henry Liu set about doing exactly the same thing they envisioned Henry would do if he were still alive and investigating the murder of a fellow journalist. Beat writers beat the bushes looking for leads, and could never be certain whether they were playing into the hands of the Information Agency. No one was to be trusted. In Taiwan, it is safer to be on the side of the Tsu-Len Gang, for there was greater loyalty among its members than there was among operatives of the Agency: the arrest of Old Duck was proof positive of that fact.

The picture of Tsu-Len Gang and the Information Agency was like a portrait of a wedding-two families standing on either side of a happy couple who joined them at the middle. Reporters uncovered the fact that Old Duck's father was a former district court judge elevated to the high court. Wu Duen, the gang's executioner, had also come from a prominent family, as had a dozen other ranking Tsu-Len lieutenants.

Tsu-Len Gang not only enjoyed deep political and family ties, they were equipped with all the latest technology and weaponry-from telecommunications to rocket launchers-most of which had been developed by the Taiwanese military. And therein lay a long and winding trail that would be more difficult to unravel than a Chinese knot.

As news of the investigation spread, contributions came from other countries detailing the relationship between Tsu-Len Gang and the Shan-Kuo and Chih-Chun gangs of Japan; Hu-Ke Gang of the Philippines; Fouteen-Ke of Hong Kong; Pei-Lin of North America, and Hwu-Chin of the United States. The gangs had reciprocity agreements like a league of nations, providing aide and assistance of every kind to members, no matter where they were and no matter where they were from.

Harder for reporters to uncover were details of the arrangement with the Information Agency which allowed Tsu-Len Gang to expand and control Taiwan like a shadow government. The lines were blurred by tracing gang members to prominent military families and Kuomintang heroes; you couldn't see the forest for the trees. Further complications arose from relating Tsu-Len gangsters to the highest ranking officials of the military, government and Information Agency. In the end, the news media dubbed the entire regime as "the family of police and gangs."

In response, the Kuomintang insisted that Taiwan was a democracy which highly regarded the rule of law. And if that was so, reporters pointed out, then why did a gang assassinate a scholar?

The quick response coming from KMT mouthpiece "The Central Daily News" claimed Henry Liu was targeted by Tsu-Len Gang after being attacked in one of Henry's TDN columns. The article supposedly was so infuriating to the gang that they put Henry's name on their death list. But reporters delving into TDN archives never found the article or the first mention of Tsu-Len—or any other gang, for that matter—and follow-ups to this claim failed to appear in "The Central Daily News."


As the proverb says, "Although things are camouflaged, paper cannot wrap fire and facts are always true." Logically, KMT's theory didn't make sense: Tsu-Len Gang never took commentaries seriously, and even if they did, Henry would not have taken them on in an article. He may have spoken his mind, but Henry knew better than to take on the gangs.

So the question remained, why put a writer to death if he had no relationship or personal feud with Tsu-Len Gang? Who was the real murderer of Henry Liu?

On 2 February 1985, "China Times" in Taipei reported that ganglord Chen Chi-Li was made an agent of the Information Agency of Taiwan two years before, and that the execution of Henry Liu had come to him from the top. Recalling the war between the KMT and Communists, a democratic politician named Wen I-Duo was assassinated, the killer was never identified, and that was the end of the story. The killer would not come forward, naturally. Similarly, the Agency would not admit to complicity in Henry's death.

And if this was so, reporters wanted to know why the Agency wanted Henry Liu dead. The first clues came to light once the cassette tapes of Old Duck were circulated. As difficult as it might be to accept, a writer could still be murdered by democratic Taiwan for having written a biography of President Jiang Jingguo.

And if this was so, reporters wanted to know if there was any security in the future for scholars, or were they all living under threat of death?

The story of Henry's murder now developed along the lines of his biography of President Jiang. By Henry's hand, the presidentand Henry's former headmaster-was a dictator who was very concerned how his ugly side was presented to the public. once Henry's book was serialized in its original form, it was the first time Jiang's facade cracked and was discussed in the streets. As Henry described, Jiang was a person who "cried when he got excited and would kill when he was cruel," and it was unfortunate for Henry that he did not understand his own observation better. when Jiang read this and other observations, he exploded in anger.

Fuel was added to the fire with Henry's book, "Memory of Wu Kuo-Chen at Age Eighty," in which he recounted Wu's just criticism of Jiang and his involvement with the Taiwanese secret police. This simply wasn't done in Taiwan: people who spoke the truth came to a bad end. Educated people endured by keeping silent, lest they lose their rank or job, or exiled as small punishment, or for severe ones, lost their lives or that of family and relatives. In the United States, no one is killed for criticism; that is what Henry had counted on, and that was where he was mistaken.

It was left to reporters to explain how Tsu-Len Gang had become the enforcers of the Information Agency. If a government could be toppled, here was the best place to start. The family portrait of police and gangs developed under the harsh glare of the media spotlight. It was widely known that the KMT had always depended on gangs to collect information in thwarting supporters of democracy. In return, gang members could be sprung from jail by the Agency. To solidify this working relationship, agents and gangsters traded places in their respective organizations.

For example, it was discovered that Tsu Kuo-Liang, a senior KMT official and Information agent was also director of "The Association of Famous Businessmen," a front for the Tsu-Len Gang. Tsu was KMT's man in Hong Kong, and after returning to Taiwan he redeemed his military rank as chief of security of the Garrison General Headquarters. While in this powerful position, Tsu extorted money from honest businessmen until his greed led to his resignation. He returned to the Association which he managed with none other than Chen Chi-Li, "Old Duck." And during the famous Project Clean-Up raid of November 1984, Tsu Kuo-Liang was nabbed with the boss.

When Old Duck and Tsu were interrogated, they advised police to be extremely cautious: "The world belongs to the father during the day and belongs to the son during the night. The Association of Famous Businessmen which you have raided is no ordinary business, it belongs to the Garrison General Headquarters."

Thus did Old Duck and TsU Kuo-Liang sketch the first details of the inner workings of "the family."

In the early days during the war against Japanese occupation, Jiang Jieshi employed two separate and distinct groups of secret agents: the Investigation & Statistics Bureau of ROC Kuomintang Central Execution Committee, abbreviated "Chung Tung," and the Investigation & Statistics Bureau of ROC Government Military Committee, abbreviated "Dring Tung." The secretary of the Central Party was head of Chung Tung, and the manager of the Military Committee oversaw Dring Tung, and these chiefs were given the title "Vice Director."

The Vice Director of Dring Tung was Dai Li, who was fiercely loyal to Jiang Jieshi. Dai Li did not allow any opposition to Jiang to survive, even though the land was no longer ruled by the concept "If the emperor wishes the subject to die, the subject must die." Democracy was the law of the land; everything follows the law—or, at least that was the way Jiang professed it to be. In all actuality, Jiang thought the law inconvenient at times, and acted at will without hindrance of law. It was Dai Li's job to execute Jiang's orders through Dring Tung.

The first notorious execution of orders by Dring Tung occurred with the arrest of the Minister of Legislature Hu Han-Ming, in May 1931. Many reasons were given for the action, but neither the military or police acting under the law executed the arrest because no legal reason existed for arresting Hu. He was merely at political odds with Jiang. And there were other infamous cases to follow, when Dring Tung apprehended Ma Ying-Chu and imprisoned him for criticizing Jiang's economic policy; Chang Shuei-Lang found himself under military law for similar offences; and Sun Li-Jen was restricted in movement by Dring Tung until his death many years later. old Jiang could not have existed without Dring Tung.

Of all the orders carried out by Dring Tung, assassination was the most risky—not because of its dangers, but because assassination is not acceptible in modern society. It should neither be used as a method to change government or as a means for the government to control the people: that was the prevalent view in Taiwan. Dring Tung, however, was willing to face condemnation for carrying out these heinous crimes out of "understanding the mind of the president and expressing loyalty."

The shocking murders of Yang Hsing-Fo and Shih Liang Tsai were blamed on the KMT, damaging the reputation of President Jiang Jieshi. Dring Tung was responsible, but their part in the crimes was unknown. Fingers were pointed at others, deflecting blame, while the KMT compelled several books to be published which praised the loyalty of Dring Tung.

The Information Agency of Taiwan was an outgrowth of Dring Tung. Owing to the history of the parent organization, it was not surprising for reporters to discover that the Agency was implicit in the murder of Henry Liu.

Hsi-Lin Wang emerged as a major role in the plot to kill Henry. Wang had been director of the Agency since 1975, and was responsible for helping agents infiltrate the United States through Taiwanese embassies and consulates. Spies were posted in major cities, usually at universities, to collect information on Taiwanese students and scholars. As an example, in 1966, Huang Chi-Ming, a Taiwanese student attending the University of Wisconsin, was arrested upon his return to Taiwan and sentenced to five years in prison for attending political meetings in the United States; that he was brother of the late mayor of Taipei was of no help to him.

More recently, in 1981, when professor Chen Wen-Chen was interrogated by police in Taiwan about his activities abroad, recordings of his lectures and private telephone conversations in the States were presented as evidence of anti-KMT sentiment. Hsi-Lin Wang's network ensured that the limitations on free speech by Taiwanese at home extended to visits abroad, and the face of KMT-styled democracy was seen in a dramatic new light.

No doubt, Henry Liu's speeches and conversations had been surveilled in the United States by Information agents. No doubt, his name appeared on the Agency's death list, which meant his elimination by agents "when chance allows." It was under this order that Wu Duen and Kuei-Sen Tung acted in removing Henry's name from the list. Notification of the deed by Old Duck to Agency Deputy Director Chen Huo-Men was simply a matter of respect and due course in this dirty business.

Reporters had a much more difficult time rooting out how the ganglord of Tsu-Len came to be enlisted by Agency Director Hsi-Lin Wang. Certainly both men's reputations were well known by the other, but Old Duck was not an easy man to find. Their initial summit meeting was arranged by general manager Lin Den-Fe of the Central Film Production Company, who maintained close ties with Tsu-Len Gang.

Director Wang and Old Duck met over dinner. The more they shared, the sorrier they were that they hadn't met sooner. Wang was impressed with the loyalty Old Duck inspired among his gang, and Old Duck was impressed by the Director's influence. Wang saw that Old Duck could be instrumental in eliminating enemies of the state beyond his reach; Old Duck saw that by forging a tie with the Agency, nothing would be impossible for Tsu-Len in Taiwan. Both agreed to be in touch again soon; film director Bai Chin-Je would be the go-between.

At their second dinner meeting, Old Duck and Director Wang were joined by Agency Vice Director I-Ming Hu. Wang dominated the conversation, making long-winded speeches about the Agency's war on Communism and the threat posed by critics of Taiwanese democracy. He sounded to Old Duck like a man covering his ass in case he, too, was the subject of surveillance. Old Duck nodded periodically in agreement with whatever Wang said, and went so far as to say that service to the government was "the most honorable commitment."

Director Wang pounced on that opening. "Then you would be willing to join the Agency?" he asked Old Duck.

Almost instinctively, Old Duck replied, "Yes, right away!"

Now it was Vic&'Director Hu's turn to chime in and promote the idea of Old Duck's enlistment. He spoke at length of his activities in Thailand and the meaning of Duty, his contributions to his country as an "anonymous hero." He was, however, not the simple man he claimed to be. HU was a devotee of Dai Li back in the days when Dring Tung was in its formative stages. It surprised no one who really knew Hu that he would one day sit one rung below the top of the Information Agency ladder.

Old Duck and Director Wang agreed that in order for the collaboration to be successful, it must be conducted at arm's length; they couldn't very well visit each other at their respective headquarters without creating a firestorm of controversy. Although Old Duck was to report directly to

Wang, Hu was to coordinate his activities and Deputy Director Chen Hou-Men was to contact him. Old Duck was given special identification and a password. And, very soon, Director Wang would have a most important assignment for his newest agent.

After a few days, Director Wang and Old Duck met a third time, under the friendlier confines of a nightclub that Tsu-Len controlled. Liquor flowed, and the Central Film Production Company sent along several beautiful young actresses for companionship. Under these influences, there was much excited conversation on a wide variety of topics, from President Jiang Jingguo to Ronald Reagan. All of which suddenly reminded Director Wang of something: the Chinese American writer Henry Liu had dared publish an unauthorized biography of President Jiang.

"Liu should be ashamed of being a graduate of Political Staff College," Wang said. "You know, in the days of Dai Li, we would've gotten rid of him quickly. But young Jiang does not approve of such action, and so we have to sit here and listen to him vociferating abroad."

All of a sudden, Old Duck roused himself. "It's okay! If you can't get rid of him, let me do it! If it's disclosed, I will be the one responsible!"

Director Wang smiled broadly and raised his glass. "Then we are waiting for your performance! Let's see if anyone dares to disgrace the president and attack the government in the future!"

"Don't worry, Director Wang. It's easy to give this kind of person a lesson."

"Maybe," the Director smiled. He drank from his glass, then added, "However, in order to fulfill your duties more efficiently, I have arranged for you to enter a short training program at Yang-Ming Shan base. Then you will be an excellent Information agent."

A few days later, Old Duck reported for induction to the training classes in Codes, Photographic Surveillance, Radio Transmissions, Transportation, and how to spot and decipher secret information from Taiwan. He received a list of contacts in Hong Kong and the United States, and viewed videos of smuggling operations. The tight schedule of classes lasted two weeks, and were closely monitored by Director Wang and Vice Director Hu.

At the end of his schooling, Old Duck was handed a thick dossier on Jiang Nang/Henry Liu. "You must kill him," Director Wang stressed. "If Henry remains alive, the problem only becomes worse." And after discussing the details, Wang and Hu decided the killing should be done by locals in San Francisco. This was no ordinary action; they should not fail.

It was obvious that the killing of Henry Liu was systematic and an order from the top, unlike typical gangland murders. It is therefore unfortunate that in the indictment handed down by the Taipei District Court the facts simply state that the crime was committed by Wu Duen, Kuei-Sen Tung and Chen Chi-Li without mentioning their motivation. Neither was there any mention of the Taiwanese government's involvement in the plot.

However, the Information Agency never realized that Old Duck could be so sneaky as to record conversations and detailed descriptions of the plot before returning to Taiwan from San Francisco. More shocking was that the cassette recordings were delivered to San Francisco police within 24 hours of Old Duck's arrest during Project Clean-Up.

The cassette tapes which Old Duck entrusted to White Wolf in case of emergency included details unknown to everyone else involved in the plot, including Wu Duen and Kuei-Sen Tung. Old Duck described how he had been enlisted by Director Wang and Vice Director Hu of the Information Agency, and how, as early as 14 September, he had travelled from Taipei to Los Angeles to hire Shai Yu-Fon and Liu Mao-Chan for the hit. Liu was indifferent to the matter—not the kind of psychopath who killed for no reason—and had been living in America too long to agree that writing a book was sufficient motive. Old Duck decided not to use locals as triggermen, but having informed Liu and Shai of the action, pressed them into service in other capacities. Old Duck had them drive him to San Francisco to begin surveillance Df the target. Old Duck was cautious not to move too quickly; a blown chance would cause great embarrassment to Director Wang and Vice Director Hu. After locating Henry's home and business, he had no choice but retreat to Los Angeles until help arrived from Taiwan.

Old Duck further recounted on tape how Tsu-Len's chief executioner, Wu Duen, was dispatched to L.A. from Taipei, and proceded to San Francisco where they awaited Kuei-Sen Tung's arrival from Taipei. And to prove that it was Wu and Tung who pulled the trigger, Old Duck described the details of Henry's murder: the garage where he was ambushed, where the bullets struck him, and the little known fact that he died with his eyes open, "as if he was not willing to leave this world."

To make sure that there would be no collusion among governments to silence the truth, Old Duck made certain that more copies of the tape made their way into the hands of publishers of Chinese-American news-papers, who were certain to have an avid interest in the murder of a jour-nalist at the hands of the KMT.

Friends and relatives of Henry Liu were saddened and angry upon read-ing the details of Old Duck's taped confession. The Cninese-American community was beginning to see the KMT for what it really was: tyranny in democratic clothing. They met on street corners, at fruit stands and grocery stores to discuss their shock and disappointment. Concern quickly turned into outrage that had no well-established avenue to vent its frustration-the Chinese community did not run to American police out of fear that they were no different from cops in Taiwan—and so they com-plained to each other.

Meanwhile, as the truth was coming to light in California, the Information Agency was busily sealing the widening cracks in their cover-up. The original plan conceived by Director Wang and Vice Director Hu called for Old Duck to be absorbed into the Agency and along with him Tsu-Len Gang. Unbeknown to Old Duck, he was also to be the scapegoat; in the event of controversy stemming from an investigation that came too close to home, Old Duck would be arrested, tried and found guilty of Henry's murder. After the noise surrounding these sensational events died down, Director Wang was to strike a deal with Old Duck that would trade his early release from prison and restoration to his former status as ganglord of Tsu-Len in exchange for his subservience to the will of the Agency. Director Wang had structured many deals like this with corrupt cops and politicians; it happened all the time.

However, the surfacing of the tapes after Old Duck's arrest caused Wang and Hu to reappraise the situation: Old Duck could not be trusted after all. Neither could the Information Agency. The tug of war between the leaders of the government's intelligence branch and the largest criminal enterprise in the world had been joined. In a conflict between the information Agency and TsuLen Gang, there was no question which side would win. Or was there?

# Chapter Four:

## Jiang Jingguo

A cursory glance at five thousand years of Chinese history shows many fine examples of notorious scoundrels rising in the political ranks.

Take, for instance, Lui Ban, the emperor of the Han dynasty, who was a scoundrel before taking power. No matter how we judge him, the fact that he was a scoundrel since childhood cannot be ignored. It seems strange that a scoundrel could climb to the seat of emperor; in some cases, perhaps it could not have happened any other way.

Without regard to personal ability, the process of seizing power has been connected with the use of gangs. At the end of the Han dynasty, Lui Ban embraced the ganglords Guan and Chang, promising that they would rule together as a triumvirate. Even Jiang Jieshi maintained close ties with ganglord Du Yue-Shen, and so it is notable that gangs have always played an important role in Chinese political history.

Opening the KMT file, it is clear that the Nationalists never gave up connections with gangs. KMT involvement with gangs began with its inception; it is said that "KMT and gangs are stacked together like two lips." Although there were times when each found it convenient to distance itself from the other, conflicts were always settled at the end, and therefore the deep rooted structure of Chinese politics can be called the "politics of gangs."

Sun Yixian had gangs raise money and shield activities in the formative stages of the KMT. They were forced to do so: the Chin dynasty used gangs to kill revolutionists; it was the revolutionists' turn to use the gangs in overthrowing the dynasty.

What about Jiang Jieshi? During his years in Shanghai, he followed Du Yueh-Shen of the Tan Gang. It was said that Jiang was short of money, and an introduction was made to the gang. It was quite easy for Jiang to join the Tan Gang because of his special identity. He did not offer gifts to Du nor perform the ritual of kneeling three times then touching the ground with his forehead nine times. The ritual was simplified for Jiang, but he still left a Tan Gang follower's name card for the record.

Jiang Jieshi later rose to a general's rank in the revolutionary corps and led his troops to victory in many battles. As he gained prominence, his followers perceived a time when allegiance to Tan Gang might pose a problem for Jiang, and they petitioned DU Yueh-Shen for the return of Jiang's Tan Gang follower's name card. Du complied with the request, and Jiang never forgot his kindness in understanding this delicate matter. Shen the rebels reached Shanghai, Jiang liberally dispensed favors to the Tan Gang.

Then again, Du Yueh-Shen was a loyal revolutionist: he slaughtered countless Communists in Shanghai in return for Jiang's favors; one hand washed the other. Since KMT was unstable, Jiang relied on the Tan Gang for information about Communists and radicals and then used gangs to carry out assassinations. Those who knew Dring Tung, the investigative branch of the military, knew that most agents were gangsters and therefore it was no surprise to learn that Old Duck had been drafted into the Information Agency. This had always been old Jiang's style, dating back to the days of the Han dynasty.

Through its close ties with Jiang Jieshi, Du was able to do whatever he wanted in Shanghai. He ran the whorehouses and drug traffic in the settlements, but in polite company Du was known as "Major Consultant," a rank signifying that he had contributed to the victory over the Communists. The cleverness of President Jiang was recognized: it was brave of him to employ gangs and bestow high rank upon their ganglords. Future generations were shy in comparison to Old Jiang: they employed gangs but lacked the courage to admit it. of course, the modern era is different. Today, the KMT claims Taiwan is a land of freedom governed by laws, and it would be contradictory to admit close ties with gangs.

While in mainland China, the KMT did not direct the gangs, vesting in them a power above police. Until today, Taiwanese gangs are able to grow large and powerful due to the indulgence of the KMT, owing to their contributions in the past.

When the KMT retreated to Taiwan after the revolution in 1949, the majority of gang members were locals. In the Fifties and Sixties, when the control of weapons was strict, gangs were limited in size. Jiang Jieshi appointed his son, Jiang Jingguo, to the military political staff in charge of the Information Agency. Wu Kuo-Chen, a close confidante of Jiang's who many years later became a biographical study for Henry Liu, was irritated by the appointment of the son by his father. Wu was well versed in the history of Jiang Jieshi and the gangs, and feared that the son would follow in the father's footsteps. Aware of Wu's misgivings, old Jiang asked his confidante what was his position on Young Jiang's appointment. Wu replied straightforwardly, "I have to help Jingguo, but I will assist him only if he works on social welfare. The world is going to blame him no matter how well he does his job. It would be best if he did not have the blood of the gangs on his hands."

Jiang Jingguo heeded the advice of his father's confidante. He was eager to establish an imposing reputation at the onset of his political career, and made it known that he did not care about gangs. Even ganglord Du Yueh-Shen sighed at the situation, recalling the good old days, and now condesc,-ondingly referring to himself as the "urinal pot, only existing when needed at night." And as power was transferred fr om old Jiang to his son, the power of Tan Gang receded.

Why, then, did Jiang Jingguo allow Tsu-Len Gang to grow large and prosper? The answer simply was that-like the Japanese-KMT also regarded gangs as an effective means to control the civilian populace. During the martial law period, KMT allowed no new political-parties or newspapers to be established. Even small seminars on public policy were illegal. During the Japanese occupation of China, they imposed a policy of "using locals to control locals," and in this-same way the KMT learned to use gangs to obtain information on influential local opposition.

Only in this manner could the KMT strengthen its control over society in a time of economic instability. Hundreds of gangs swamped Taipei in the mid-Sixties, like bamboo shoots after the rain.

The single most significant reason why gangs proliferated in Taiwan was due to their close connection with the Information Agency. To hide this fact, the Agency periodically sacrificed a scapegoat: and Agency bureau chief in Taipei was charged with consorting with Tsu-Len Gang and was forced to resign, was tried in court and sentenced to jail. The case received major news coverage, but all the while the other bureau chiefs were free to carry on business as usual with Tsu-Len.

The public was aware of three large gangs in Taiwan. Other than Tsu-Len, there was Shi-Hai of Taipei and Shi-Bei of Kao Shiung. Tsu-Len was the quickest to develop, primarily because many of its members were sons of soldiers who retreated from the mainland after the revolution and supplied intelligence to the Information Agency. No sooner than the KMT established a hold in Taiwan, Jiang Jieshi had to worry about opposition, and Tsu-Len was put to work ferreting out the competition.

The arrangement between the KMT and the gangs has continued to the present day. The Hung Men Gang of Chung-Li boasts several branches, and at their Chen-I Hall of Lung-Gung, KMT emblems are displayed alongside a portrait of Jiang Jieshi. Among their members, a "custodian" is a colonel from the Political Staff College. Ask him why the

Hung Men Gang acts without fear of retribution and he replies that the gang operates in connection with police and the Information Agency. The gangs and the KMT are like sworn brothers. This is an "open secret" from the Taiwanese public.

Jiang Jingguo was able to succeed as president simply by reflecting the policies of his father. In the Eighties, however, the world trend towards democracy and freedom underscored a new push for reform in Taiwan. Jiang Jingguo decided that his sons would not follow in his footsteps: his oldest son, Jiang Hsaio-Won, was a vagabond infected with syphilis, and the other two sons weren't up to the challenges of the presidency. They remained in the business world. Jiang Hsaio-Wu ran the "Voice of Free China" radio network, but only until his father made him Secretary of the National Security Council.

In the complicated intelligence system teeming with high ranking generals, Jiang Hsaio-Wu was unable to revise the way things worked. He had no choice but to learn to work with Tsu-Len Gang to improve his reputation, and became head of the National Security Council while rising in the gang ranks at the same time.

Only through Tsu-Len Gang was Jiang Hsaio-Wu able to control the media in Taiwan. The gang owned the entertainment business, and crossed paths with Jiang at Free China radio. When Jiang Hsaio-Wu was appointed Secretary of the National Security Council, he fell back on his long-standing working relationship with TsU-Len Gang in bringing newspapers under his control.

This is how Old Duck and Tsu-Len became involved with the Information Agency plot to murder Henry Liu, through Jiang Hsaio-Wuls connections. Long before Old Duck was approached by Agency Director Wang and Vice Director Hu, he had served time in Green Island Prison. Upon release, he did not return to the gang right away since his legitimate business concerns needed his attention. But Jiang Hsaio-Wu had other plans: he wanted Old Duck back at the helm of

Tsu-Len to recruit new informants on the Taiwanese Independence Movement who threatened Jiang's father's regime.

Old Duck was unmoved by the plight of the Jiangs. He'd had enough of political subterfuge, he was getting too old for this business. Jiang Hsaio-Wu did not give up easily. Through an intermediary, he requested a meeting with Old Duck, which was held at the House of Freedom in Taipei. Located near the home of a former president, the House was used for KMT activities. Tsu-Len enjoyed its use as one of the perks from the KMT. It was also through the KMT that Old Duck published Mei-Hua magazine, and through this maze of connections the Jiangs decided that Old Duck would make the perfect Information agent.

Of course, President Jiang Jingguo was not about to make these arrangements personally with Old Duck. His son, Jiang Hsaio-Wu, laid the groundwork at their initial meeting at the House of Freedom by persuading Old Duck to reactivate his position as lord of Tsu-Len Gang. Then the Information Agency took over, sending in Director Wang and Vice Director Hu to flesh out the plot to kill Henry Liu. This is how it is done in Taiwan carefully and in progressive stages. "To achieve whatever the leader wants without spilling a word, to think what the leader thinks and to worry what the leader worries," as the old saying goes.

The plot to kill Henry Liu—from Old Duck's induction to the Information Agency, his leaving Taiwan and going abroad, the hiring of hitmen, the actual murder, and escape back home-was all part of a plan formed by the Information Agency. Out of continuing fear for the emergence of opposition parties, the KMT continued to control elections through the gangs: killing a political writer outside Taiwan was meant to be a cautionary warning to others that criticism of President Jiang Jingguo would not be tolerated, even while denying the involvement of the government at every level.

Political observers with a sharp eye for the manner in which gang leaders and corrupt government officials are arrested and imprisoned only to be released and restored to power wondered at the Project Clean-Up arrests of November 1984. In the wake of the Liu murder investigation, the action certainly seemed politically expedient, rather than a crackdown on gang violence.

Other cases of corruption came to light at this same time. A KMT sponsored candidate who won a seat in Taipei's third district turned out to be a gang leader. Constituents were hard pressed to complain because their new councilor was more efficient than local police at solving crimes: robberies which formerly went uninvestigated by police were solved in three days by the new councilman's gang connections. And in the fifth district, another gangster candidate lost the election when his gambling and prostitution connections were exposed by a KMT committee member. The gangster was also a KMT candidate, however, and the party discharged the committee member who blew the whistle. Observers were stupefied by the incredible number of gangsters who doubled as civic-minded politicians in Taiwan.

At its most flagrant, the KMT's election rigging was illustrated by the case of a gangster elected to the legislature in 1970. After his election, he never attended sessions of the Legislative Assembly and no one was aware of his existence. At the end of his three-year term, the KMT and local gangs got him re-elected to a second term.

In 1980, the KMT overlooked Hung Wen-Dong as a potential legislator. Cultivating a strong relationship with gangs, however, earned him a KMT nomination in 1983. Numerous gangsters threw their support behind Hung, and he was elected by a wide margin. By the above cases, it was obvious to observers that the KMT and the gangs could not easily survive without each other, another batch of "open secrets" in Taipei political circles.

The cooperation between the KMT and the gangs was a twoway street. KMT had the power, but the gangs had the money and the influence. The gangs could buy an election, and as long as the KMT allowed them to profit from illegal activities, the circle turns. Voters caught up in the middle of this mess had no choice but to take the bribes, otherwise "the knife goes in clean and comes out red." Who could resist such an offer?

What prevented the opposition from utilizing gangs to win seats? The KMT assertion that any gang backing the opposition would be wiped out. on the other hand, gangsters who aided KMT candidates continued to operate under the shelter of the KMT. Why replace one corrupt official with another?

All of which caused political observers to pose one final question: Under the leadership of such a corrupt government, how could the people of Taiwan enjoy freedom and democracy?

# Chapter Five:

## *Jiang Hsalio-Wu*

The idea for Project Clean-Up of the Tsu-Len Gang was hatched early in the morning of 12 November 1984, the day before it was implemented. The concept originated with the National Security Council, under the auspices of Secretary Jiang Hsaio-Wu, who reported events as they unfolded to his father, President Jiang Jingguo. Owing to the close working relationship that the KMT and Tsu-Len Gang had enjoyed, an attack by one against the other seemingly served to only weaken both.

The National Security Council's motive was clear, to distance the government from the gangsters who had murdered Henry Liu, for in the months following Project Clean-Up, American authorities announced that suspects in the case were tied to the Tsu-Len Gang of Taiwan. It was all designed as a smokescreen, to keep observers guessing at the identity of the culprits. Because the Project was also aimed at Information agents, it was even more difficult to understand. Was the KMT really cleaning house, or was it covering its tracks?

The KMT could point to a National Security Council directive to the Taipei police—dated ten months before the Liu murder and Project Clean-Up—to eliminate all known gathering places of gangs, owing to an increase in violence. And from May until September, the kMT allowed amnesty to gang members who retired and went straight: 3,000 gangsters from 651 gangs registered; the KMT emphasized that Project Clean-Up was an extension of a policy that had been in place, designed to strike at those hold-outs from amnesty.

The Project Clean-Up actions that followed the November 1984 sweep of Tsu-Len Gang netted more than 300 gang members. Chen Chi-Li was at top of the list, along with Henry Liu's assassin, Wu Duen, and the staff of Old Duck's magazine, "Hua-Mei Report." The names of 38 other gangsters were included, so that the action appeared in the guise of a citywide cleansing. For the most part, the reaction among Taipei citizens was overwhelmingly positive. only political wiseguys had reservations that there were other implications to the arrests.

There were some critics who thought the police action signalled a transfer of power, from father to son, from Jiang Jingguo to Jiang Hsaio-Wu. Critics could remember a time four years earlier when President Jiang held a KMT meeting to put his son's name forward as his successor. Traditionally, the act of succession is slow—as it had been in the case of Jiang Jieshi handing the baton to Jiang Jingguo—and is always preceded by a cleansing. In other words, the need to clean society, the party, and its opposition in order to prevent instability during the transition of power.

Thus, in order to have a clean society, it is necessary to sweep the gangs to avoid their being used by dissidents. Speeches by dissidents must be suppressed and their organizations broken apart. Critics like Henry Liu must be dealt with harshly, lest their ideas poison the political water. As part of the cleansing, "The American China Times" newspaper was aborted, and the off-party Public Political Council was disbanded.

Jiang Hsaio-Wuls "Project Clean-Up" was in many respects no different from a cleansing enacted by his father thirty years before. Before rising to president of Taiwan, Jiang Jingguo held the position of Director of the Information Department of the President's office. He supervised the "Information Collection Committee of Taiwan," which controlled the intelligence system, and when the time neared for Jiang Jieshi to annoint his son as successor, they devised a "Project Clean-Up" to usher in the new era.

Jiang Hsaio-Wu had risen in government in the manner of his father— first as Executive Secretary of the National Security Council (on a level with the Minister of Defense and the General of Garrison Headquarters), and then as head of the intelligence system. But the rising generation was superior to its ancestor: whereas it had taken Jiang Jingguo ten years to build his system and defeat Wu Kuo-Chen and Chen Chen, it only took Jiang Hsaio-Wu a year and a half to squelch his detractors.

After another four or five years of manuevering, Jiang Hsaio-Wu grew even stronger. Not only was the Investigation Bureau under his command, he also had a special office set in Taiwan Garrison General Headquarters. It could be said that he controlled the two main pillars of the intelligence system, and as such he could attack as well as defend any political situation. In July 1984, Chief General Hou Bou-Chen held a banquet for Jiang Hsaio-Wu where ten-other generals toasted him like stars to the moon. As the generals fell in line behind him, Jiang believed succession would be smooth.

Now that Jiang Hsaio-Wu had the essential power to succeed, Project Clean-Up and the murder of Henry Liu were just a matter of details. Jiang Jingguo was enjoying his last few days, believed the succession must be implemented without delay and thus tolerated his son's behaviour.

The National Security Council was at the top of the KMT's eight intelligence systems. It took charge of the Investigation Bureau, Information Agency, Taiwan Garrison General Headquarters, General Political Warfare Department, Headquarters of military Police, Department of Police Administration, and Headquarters of the Central Party. Every intelligence organization was under the control of the National Security Council but substantially suppressed each other for a balance check; there were frequent jurisdictional conflicts.

During the gang amnesty from the end of May until the end of September 1984, all eight intelligence systems were dedicated to creating the clean-up list. After the list was submitted to the National Security Council, it appeared that the information was incomplete, owing to arrangements between certain gangsters and the particular system they had relations with. In order to cure the defects due to such biases, Jiang Hsaio-Wu took over the Information Agency and eliminated all disloyal systems officials.

The front line of Project Clean-Up was made up of Information agents, and standing behind them was Jiang Hsaio-Wu. His National Security Council delivered marching orders in sealed envelopes to police captains. Inside each envelope were four slips of paper: a search warrant enabling police to go anywhere, an arrest warrant enabling police to arrest anyone, a list of names, and an address where they could be found. The captains were stunned; they would be arresting friends and partners.


Chen Chi-Li (Old Duck) was to Jiang Hsaio-Wu what Tan ganglord Du Yueh-Shen had been to Jiang Jieshi. Old Duck had been a soldier in Tsu-Len Gang for a dozen years before rising atop an empire of restaurants, nightclubs and entertainment-related businesses. The most remarkable enterprise in Old Duck's conglomerate was "Hua-Mei Report," a magazine geared toward the entertainment industry—the threat of exposing the private lives of wealthy people and famous stars was a lucrative source of hush money. Through blackmail, Old Duck infiltrated the highest levels of Taiwanese society.

Old Duck was "forever fortifying the gang" by mending fences with the KMT and the intelligence system. If he made only one mistake in this process, Old Duck showed the world an arrogant face, as if his-connections made him invincible. what angered his associates in the intelligence system was his flaunting the murder of Henry Liu as a contract only he could fill, that there was no one in all of Taiwan-with his unique ability to call down thunder from the heavens. Thus, Old Duck was thought of as the proverbial loose cannon, and was targeted in Project Clean-Up before his big mouth boasted of Henry Liu's assassination once too often.

"Seal your mouths completely," Information Agency Deputy Director Chen Hou-Men had warned Liu's assassins, "even to parents and wives, and you need not fear anything from us." Unfortunately for Old Duck, he had not bothered to remember this admonition.

The staff of Old Duck's "Hua-Mei Report" was also targeted in Project Clean-Up because its publisher, Yu Shiang-Shen, was known as the director of the underworld information network, the shadowy counterpart of the KMVs intelligence system. Yu received protection from his father-in-law who was president of "Ming-Tsu Evening News," had long been a legislator of Tseh-Chiang province, and had a good relationship with Jiang Jingguo. Yu was friendly with Jiang's sons, however, he failed to realize that as the heir to his father's throne, Jiang HsaioWu could not be treated with the same familiarity as his siblings. Jiang Hsaio-Wu was accorded the respect of the older generation.

Tsu Kuo-Liang of the "Famous Businessmen's Club" was swept up with Chen Chi-Li and Wu Duen. He, too, had led a double life as Deputy Chief of Taiwan's Security Department of the Garrison General Headquarters and as a ganglord. He teamed with Old Duck in ruling Tsu-Len Gang, but once made the mistake of offending Jiang Hsaio-Wu, which was not forgotten. Thus, the lofty excuse to purify the underworld was also a thinly veneered desire of Jiang's to eliminate Tsu Kuo-Liang.

Project Clean-Up hauled in three members of Tsu-Len Gang who were also police officials—Lu Chun, Dong Chen-Chun and Chi Que-Chen. Lu and Dong were confined while interrogators grilled Chi for six hours. He was accused of hiding suspects and weapons but was later released when no evidence was found. As Chi later related, "I have served in the police force for thirty years. I never thought the guys at the top would believe the trap that others set for me. No matter what, I am still a two-star three-line officer of Kaoshiung City Police Station. These interrogators from security did not show me any respect. I feel very useless."

If Chi Que-Chen suffered no worse, it was because of the Jiang policy of "no punishment for police officials," so that disgraced cops would not completely lose face. No matter how corrupt, ranking police officers were never publicly humiliated. Chi was the exception to this rule; his dignity was sacrificed in order to heighten the prestige of Jiang Hsaio-Wu.

Chi Que-Chen's arrest alerted his friends in Kaoshiung City. No important figures were arrested there, when news of Chi's arrest reached t hem before Intelligence agents arrived. one key figure who eluded capture was Shih Yuan-Yuan, who occupied a unique position with both the government and the underworld. He was called "The Commander of A Thousand Years," and was considered untouchable by police chiefs far and wide. It was Jiang Hsaio-Wuls plan to gain control over Shih's mob by appointing him director of Keeliung Harbor Police and moving in once Shih's power in the underworld diminished.

The riskiest element to the success of Project Clean-Up actually came from outside Taiwan: if San Francisco police cracked the Liu case, the KMT would be embarrassed if they could not produce the murderers. And the KMT believed that the FBI would soon add the names Chen Chi-Li, Wu Duen and Kuei-Sen Tung to its Most Wanted list. If the murderers were apprehended in Project Clean-Up, KMT could control their statements and negotiate with authorities in the United States. That is the only reason why Project Clean-Up was expedited within 24 hours of its inception, in a race with the FBI.

When Old Duck's tapes surfaced and his identity as an Information agent was made known, Project Clean-Up began to fall apart. The FBI noted that progress in the case might have been swifter had the KMT cooperated with them, but as the ChineseAmerican community in San Francisco pointed out, the KMT is reluctant to cooperate in the investigation of plots it is secretly involved in. Chen Chi-Li, Wu Duen and Kuei-Sen Tung were now openly known as suspects in the murder of Henry Liu.

"The San Francisco Times" reported on 3 December 1984 that Chen Chi-Li of Tsu-Len Gang had departed from Taiwan to California on 27 September with one million dollars. His return to Taiwan six days later was also documented. According to Old Duck's associates, the money purportedly was for legitimate investments in the States, but the money was never deposited in the U.S. The article went on to explain that Old Duck had been nabbed on the first night of Project Clean-Up, shortly after his return to Taiwan. And that, said The Times, was an odd coincidence.

The initial response to this report from the Taiwanese intelligence system was that they had no knowledge of the Liu murder beforehand and that clues were detected only after the arrest of Old Duck on unrelated charges. They claimed to have contacted U.S. authorities immediately with the information, but The Times was unable to verify that claim.

To the contrary, the FBI encountered layers of obstacles when requesting contact with the suspects or obtaining their files and fingerprints from Taipei police. The FBI claimed that Taiwan refused to allow contact with the suspects, and refused to extradite them or provide any information. The odd coincidence of Project Clean-Up coming on the heels of the Liu murder coupled with Taiwan's uncooperative attitude with the FBI investigation painted a dark picture of the KMT.

Within 24 hours of Project Clean-Up's initial sweep, a series of anonymous telephone tips poured into the offices of off-party publications claiming that Tsu-Len Gang was responsible for Liu's death, and that the gang would make the truth known as a result of the crackdown.

Project Clean-Up folded after seven days of arrests. occasionally, reports came out that someone else was arrested, but these turned out to be minor players. Most of the big names had been captured. Warrants did not exist for many others who might've been caught and those who were collared without warrants soon walked for insufficient evidence. This was a hot topic of gossip throughout Taiwan.

Project Clean-Up then bogged down in a rather bizarre turn of events: as news of the arrests reached a climax, reports from concerned citizens flooded police precincts containing tips on gang activity which typically turned out to be exaggerations and personal feuds. In a country where accusations of practically anybody and everybody could be easily believed, the police were having an impossible time following the leads pouring in by the boatload.

Lastly, the one factor which spelled doom for Project Clean-Up was the age-old connection between cop and robber. At certain levels, these confederacies were like family ties and many gangsters were immune from arrest. Even when the KMT sought to set an example by arresting a few retired police directors who shielded gangsters, the plan backfired when the public was shocked to learn the existence of these cover-ups. Worse yet, these arrests failed to frighten other active policemen guilty of the same crime. The further Project Clean-Up went, the broader it grew until the KMT had no choice but to put an end to it before it toppled the entire regime.

# Chapter Six:

## *Fountain*

8 April 1985

The whole world watched as the Taipei District Court reached a decision in the case of Henry Liu's murderers. Proceedings had been heard by a panel of three judges who unanimously decided that Chen Chi-Li and Wu Duen were guilty of Murder. The defendants did not appear in court; the judgment was read to them by the director of the detention center where they had been entombed.

Chen Chi-Li was sentenced to life in prison and deprived of all rights for his role in Henry's murder. In addition, another three years were tacked on to his sentence for the illegal possession of weapons. Wu Duen also received a life sentence for his role in the murder and was deprived of all rights. Added to that was a two-year sentence for gang-related activities. The sentences were to be served concurrently, and under Taiwanese law, a prisoner serving a life sentence who behaved could expect to be paroled within ten years. Under these circumstances, observers couldn't help but wonder at the sentence Old Duck and Wu would have received had they been extradited to the United States.

A committee formed by the Liu family of friends, relatives, journalists, scholars and other concerned Chinese-Americans banded together and called for justice. Their aims were clear, they had two goals: the first was to demand a full inquest into the Liu case, the second to appeal to the U.S. federal government to protect the rights and freedoms of Chinese-Americans by demanding Henry's killers be extradited to the United States.

The Chinese-American community had wearied of waiting for President Reagan to denounce Taiwan's act of international terrorism, as part of his diplomatic policy. Reagan had righteously condemned the killer of two Americans on a Kuwaiti airliner, yet Henry's murder at home in California was being overlooked. It was left to the committee of concerned ChineseAmericans to suppose that a cover-up of sorts was firming up in Washington.

Four months before the verdict was handed down by the Taipei District Court, Taipei officials admitted the involvement of the Information Agency in Henry Liu's death, bringing waves of reaction in American political circles. California legislators called for extradition, lest Taiwan become a harbor for international terrorism. The State Department and FBI claimed that all efforts to extradite Wu Duen and Chen Chi-Li had failed thus far, leaving the matter to the Diplomatic Affairs Committee in the U.S. House of Representatives to issue a formal request to Taiwan for extradition. The next step depended on Taiwan's response.

The KMT refused to extradite Wu Duen and Chen Chi-Li on a technicality: there was no extradition treaty between Taiwan and the United States. According to international law, the KMT pointed out, any country has the right to expel foreigners, but without an extradition treaty, no country was compelled to hand over one of its citizens to another country. Diplomatic ties alone did not form legal grounds for extradition, although many friendly nations routinely complied with extradition requests without treaties in force.

Taiwan's refusal was also predicated on the concept of Equality Between Two Nations, that Taiwanese law specified that a nation requesting extradition should return the favor or the request shall be refused. And Taiwan pointed out many instances where Taiwanese white collar criminals had fled to America, and the U.S. failed to comply with extradition requests from Taiwan. Extradition without a treaty could happen theoretically, the KMT said, to keep peace and order in this world; all countries have the responsibility to extradite criminals, but at the very least, obstacles in the law based upon the principle of Equality could be reasonably expected. The extradition of Chen Chi-Li and Wu Duen was not absolutely impossible, the KMT hinted, there were precedents. The question was, what does Taiwan really want in return for its cooperation?

From the legal point of view, Taiwan was well within its rights to refuse extradition to the United States. From a political level, refusal not only caused chaos from critics but threatened Taiwan's economic dependence on the U.S. To extradite Chen and Wu would demonstrate Taiwan's friendliness, unless the rumors of the KMT's involvement in Henry's murder were true. Considering the complexity and sensitivity of the affair on a political level, some critics thought Taiwan would be best served by extraditing Chen and Wu as a diplomatic-courtesy.

Just as the KMT got stuck on the legal aspect of extradition, claims that "an American had been killed on American soil" resounded in the halls of the witness conference for Henry's murder in Marin County, California. Almost every speaker at the meeting repeated the phrase like a mantra, and growing public concern pushed the U.S. government to take action.

Under a consensus, the Pacific Team of the U.S. House of Representatives passed a resolution requesting Taiwan to extradite Chen Chi-Li and Wu Duen, emphasizing that unless Taiwan complied they would be suspected of taking part in a cover-up. Congress went even further, stating that formal relations with Taiwan would be harmed, particularly regarding the sale of weapons.

In support of the resolution, Rep. Ritchie of Iowa and Rep. Fountain of California also pointed out that if the Taiwanese government was proven to be involved in the Liu murder, the State Department should consider eliminating Taiwanese consulates and expelling ROC representatives. Fountain went so far as to condemn President Reagan's failure to push the issue, which he said showed an insensitivity to Asian Americans and seriously damaged human rights in the United States. As Japanese blood flowed in his veins, Fountain added, "Henry Liu was an American citizen like any other. If he had had white skin, the U.S. government would have handled the case differently."

"Stop terrorism," Fountain concluded, but his request received only a curious silence from the Justice Department. In followup letters to the Justice Department on the heels of his speech, Fountain urged, "Asian Americans generally lack confidence in the U.S. system of justice. If Henry Liu had been Polish, killed by an agent from Poland, or a white American journalist murdered by Iranian terrorists, the situation would have been totally different."

"On one hand, the U.S. government reproaches terrorist attacks on Americans, but on the other hand, domestic terrorism is being ignored," Fountain continued. "We cannot tolerate Taiwan becoming a shelter for murderers."

"I am disgusted that crimes can be committed on our land by agents from another country, and then run back to their own country for protection under their government. Whomever commits crimes on American soil should be judged under U.S. laws."

Largely on the merit of Fountain's pleas, the House of Representatives requested an extradition of the suspects from Taiwan.

Almost as soon as the request was formally made, speculation that Taipei would deny extradition was bantered by congressmen who posed questions of what would follow. Denial of a congressional request was unprecedented, but lacking a formal diplomatic relationship with Taiwan, all Congress could do was suspend relations and invite ROC diplomats to leave the United States. under these conditions, the FBI might never learn the truth of Henry Liu's murder and the extent to which KMT officials were involved.

International law expert Michael Glenon, author of a report on the secret activities of Taiwanese agents in America, suggested that Congress modify its Taiwan Relation Laws to restrain the activities of Taiwanese agents on American soil. Speaking as a law professor from Cincinnati University, Glenon pointed out that since no formal diplomatic ties existed between the U.S. and Taiwan, the ROC diplomatic right of exemption was not on par with other nations enjoying full diplomatic relations, going so far as to recommend a suspension or cancellation of the Relation Laws.

Glenon also reminded congressmen of the Weapon Control Act, which provided that the U.S. government could suspend or cancel the exportation of weapons to Taiwan. If Taiwan depended on the U.S. for its arsenal—spending one billion dollars per year-it seemed unlikely to Glenon that the Taiwanese would risk a threat to its national security merely to mask the identity of two murderers.

Underscoring the threat to suspend diplomatic relations and arms sales, the Tax Committee weighed in with the threat of eradicating the sliding scale of customs duties which were liberally tipped in Taiwan's favor.

Clearly, the KMT government had a great deal of serious consequences to consider. Intellectuals debated the KMT's stance in the newspaper's, and the prevailing view was that the government should be open and flexible. While everyone understood that Taiwanese laws did not allow for the extradition of its citizens as a matter of sovereignty,the killing of an American citizen on U.S. soil encroached upon U.S. sovereignty and extradition of the suspects was deemed the proper action. At least, that was the opinion of Taiwanese editorial pages.

The KMT, however, held a different view: the illegality of extradition was an absolute right of Taiwanese citizens. only when this defense appeared to isolate the government from its people did the KMT spell out a convoluted course of action that must be followed in setting its extradition laws aside: first, the U.S. would have to petition the Ministry of Foreign Affairs in Taiwan. And then the Minister of Foreign Affairs would notify the ministry of Justice, who then would procede to the District Prosecutor's office. The prosecutor would require 24 hours to interrogate the suspects and upon completion of his report would file it with the District Court. The court would give the parties 60 days to respond, and another 30 days to render a decision. After the decision was handed down to the Minister of Foreign Affairs via the Minister of Justice, it would be delivered to President Jiang by way of the Minister of Administration. And, at this rate, the KMT estimated that the extraditions of Old Duck and Wu Duen would take no less than 120 days.

One hundred twenty days was too long for the urgent need of Henry's case. Even then, there was no guarantee that extradition would succeed the torturous route through the court and three ministries. Anyone with even the most limited knowledge of KMT manuevers knew it was highly unlikely that a gang leader would be handed over to American authorities.

While a suspension of the rules was being debated in Taipei, the Congress of the United States forged ahead in building up an extradition treaty with Taiwan. Once the treaty was signed, the U.S. promised to extradite all Taiwanese economic fugitives who had siphoned off huge fortunes and fled to America, but in the 6-week interim it would take to clear the committee on Foreign Affairs, Taiwan was requested to fully cooperate in the Liu case and send Old Duck and Wu Duen to California for trial.

The KMT response was firm in its rejection of congressional pressure: Old Duck and Wu Duen were to be tried in Taiwan for the murder of Henry Liu. The U.S. Senate was quick to counter. Senator Richie, speaking on behalf of the committee on Foreign Affairs, said, "Our concern is not who killed Henry Liu, but who ordered the murder. Trying the suspects in Taiwan will make it harder to discover the truth."

However, just one day after Senator Richie made his declaration, Taipei announced that the KMT had moved quickly to resolve the case and hastily convened a trial. And before the U.S. Senate could issue further reaction, the Taiwanese government declared that the suspects in the murder of Henry Liu had been found guilty and sentenced to life in prison.

Back in Washington, D.C., the State Department notified the Liu family that the truth of Henry's murder might have to wait twenty years to come to light.

# *Chapter Seven*

## *Townspeople*

Henry Liu died so suddenly, so unbelievably, that it was shocking, sad, and inflamed enormous anger from the Chinese communities here and abroad. It was obvious that he was assassinated for political reasons. People who heard about the hit were stunned by it, and promptly set out in search of the truth. The case was not without precedent; a growing list of similar executions had occurred in Taiwan ever since the Revolution of 1911:

March 1913. Sung Hsaio-Jen of the KMT was assassinated under Yuan Shih-Kai's direction in Shanghai because he was an advocate of the cabinet system.

January 1931. Seven Chinese avant-garde writers were arrested and executed in Shanghai.

June 1933. Yang Hsin-Fou was assassinated in Shanghai. His crime was being director of the Chinese Protective Human Rights Association.

November 1934. Shi Liang-Tsi of the most famous newspaper in Shanghai, "Sheng News," was assassinated for publishing criticisms of the KMT.

July 1946. The patriot Lee Kon-Poo was assassinated in Kwin-Ming along with several well-known writers and professors for their human rights activities.

June 1948. A professor at Taiwan National University was assassinated in his home.

And the list goes on.

Beginning in 1949, a dozen quiet years passed during which the people were lulled into thinking that life could be enjoyed in harmony…until more brutal incidents exploded, starting with the slaughter of a civil rights lawyer's family and the murder of a math professor who had returned to Taiwan from the U.S. for a visit, and ending with the ambush of Henry Liu at his home in California. It was a long bloody road crossing time and space.

Ever since Henry's murder in October 1984, reverberations from Taiwan have continued unabated. on 2 November, a reporter from "The New York Times" published an account, "Critic of Taiwanese Leader Killed; Chinese in America Terrified," which became the basis for his book, "Life In China." The publication of The Times article caused a Chinese-American student at Berkeley to write a letter to the editor explaining that fellow students who had criticized the KMT were in fear for their lives. what is more, he noted with regret, to follow Henry's example by recording Chinese history with a strong sense of righteousness, to seek truth without betraying one's own conscience, was vanishing from the earth.

We cry for the senseless act of violence. We cry for the stupidity of humanity.

A crowd of more than 400 mourners attended a funeral service for Henry Liu at Lee-An funeral parlor in San Francisco's Chinatown. The presence of reporters from newspapers and tv stations provoked anger in the midst of solemnity and sadness.


Henry's portrait hung in the hallway. He was laid out in a neat tan suit, and looked as if he were in quiet contemplation. The mortician had done a masterful job restoring his face. Arranged around his coffin were garlands and wreaths of flowers with condolences from Time magazine,

"China Express," "China Broadcast," "Taiwan and the World," and the student association from the University of California at Berkeley. The People's Republic of China in San Francisco sent a delegation who lauded Henry as "one living abroad with a heart of unifying the mother country, commenting with a righteous pen as a hero of the time." The mourning association wrote a salutory couplet, promising to "wash Henry's tomb-stone with tears of sadness."

After the ceremony, mourners filed past the open coffin for a parting glance of their jade warrior as orchids were draped over him; an orchestra played, a procession of thirty cars passed through Chinatown for the cremation at Cypress Cemetery-there might have been a hundred more, had not Henry's friends stayed away out of fear for their own safety. Surely, the KMT had spies about.

Henry's assassination shook San Francisco to its core, the shock waves creating an earthquake overseas. Reports were filed with every Taiwanese newspaper: left-wing publications pointed a finger at the KMT; KMT papers asked everyone to remain calm. News releases out of Washington, D.C. mentioned Information Agency participation in the plot, while the Chinese Culture Research Association held that "as long as writers hold a conscientious heart without encroaching upon the territory of the law, they should not be harmed regardless of the content of their writing."

Left-wing publishers drove home the point that Henry's murder was meant to be a cautionary sign to Chinese-Americans. Hong Kong's "Wide Scope" wrote that "If the Information Agency could infiltrate the United States, why couldn't they do the same in Hong Kong?" And fear spread from Taiwan to the mainland; every Chinese circle was concerned about Henry's death.

Taiwan's two off-party magazines were forbidden to comment on Henry's death. Meanwhile, mainland China reacted enthusiastically. The director of the People's Republic of China in San Francisco personally appeared at the Liu home to express his condolences. The PRC in China dispatched messengers to Henry's family in Jing-iiang. And the PRC strongly urged the United States to investigate, probe, arrest and punish the murderers in accordance with the law.

On 5 November 1984, more than 200 of Henry's friends assembled at National Political Hall in Beijing to denounce Taiwan and demand justice. A message to Henry's widow was drafted and sent by wire:

"We were surprised and angered at the incidence of Henry being murdered cruelly, therefore a mourning assembly was held today at Beijing. We send our warmest regards.

"Henry was righteous, talented, and his writing has widely affected Chinese overseas: at the peak of his years Henry encountered devilish-hands, and we strongly reproach those underground members for using low tactics and committing the crime of murder. We are determined to support Chinese in the U.S. and Chinese-American request for justice, will ask the U.S. to solve the case and severely punish the murderers, so the truth can be known. Henry's blood will not be shed for naught."

The official Taiwanese response to Henry's death was strangely cold; there were no representatives sent to the Liu home or to the funeral, nor any words of condolence mailed to Henry's widow. Taipei's office in Washington, D.C. relayed to the Daly City police that Taiwan would do its very best to solve the case and act to better protect the lives of its citizens abroad. It was left to Henry's friends to point out that mainland China seemed to be Henry's friend while his homeland appeared distant.

The Taiwanese Townspeople Association held a demonstration on 26 January 1985, to protest the KMT's involvement in Henry's death. Henry's widow attended a press conference that was aimed at stirring up a country-wide support for the association's human rights agenda. Striking a chord of response with neighboring provinces was an important breakthrough for the association. Historically, the Taiwanese believed that surrounding provinces were a hotbed of KMT activity, while the provincial point of view was that the Taiwanese descriminated against them. There was a constant bickering, each holding fast to their unwavering convictions. The Taiwanese Public Relations Association sought to break the deadlock by promoting the idea that all Chinese citizens are entitled to the same political benefits regardless of their province, and that Chinese abroad should fight for democracy, freedom and human rights, working as "one heart" towards the common goal.

The Taiwanese Townspeople-although outspoken—had never been involved in a case like Henry's murder. The history of their movement was to operate like a booster club in support of progress, whether it was an arms agreement with the U.S. or arranging tours for groups of business-men to stimulate trade. And in encouraging Taiwanese exiles to return to their homeland, the Townspeople proclaimed that their government must do all that was in its power to protect the freedom of its citizenry. All of which underscored the urgency of getting to the bottom of the Liu case.

The KMT never figured on the Taiwanese Townspeople's involvement in currying public opinion. This called for a change in strategy, before the Townspeople could unite Chinese abroad. There were signs that the Townspeople were being heard in the U.S., where the Democratic Freedom Alliance launched a "free speech campaign," citing Henry's case as evidence that the rights of Chinese everywhere was endangered.

There were indications that the efforts of the Townspeople were also being noticed elsewhere. Such news naturally reached England, the homeland of Henry's professor, Sir Michael Lindsay. Sir Michael was at home when Henry was murdered, attending the Upper House of Parliament for discussions about Hong Kong. He received press clip-pings from "The Washington Post" that Henry's daughter mailed, and his angry reaction to the news of Henry's death was published in the British press.

"How could Jiang Jingguo be so stingy as to not be able to tolerate a few criticisms?" Sir Michael posed. "If he can't hear criticism, he might as well leave the pedestal."

Sir Michael's Chinese-born wife also recalled meeting Henry as a stu-dent ten years earlier, when he visited their home and often chatted with the professor until after midnight. Speaking as a Chinese expatriate, she added that the KMT was creating a rising discontent among the expat community. Chinese-Americans and those in Britain, she said, had been awakened to the KMT's oppression and no longer wanted to keep their opinions to themselves.

Henry's death had not only touched Chinese circles in the U.S., Taiwan, Hong Kong and mainland China, but had gone beyond Chinese societies to the rest of the world; that the story had such long legs was not to be expected by the KMT. Now it was a matter of Taiwan saving face: the Ministry of Justice announced a new investigation into the murder of Henry Liu.

# Chapter Eight

## *The Seven Letters*

In the early days of 1985, the government of Taiwan engaged in a "Battle of Canvassing" on the floor of the U.S. Congress. The KMT was in a fight with congressmen who were very concerned about the Liu case, and efforts to smooth over the incident was made in both the American and Taiwanese media.

The Ministry of Justice, as promised, arranged for a delegation of Americans to travel to Taipei for an investigation. The itinerary was carefully orchestrated to create every appearance of KMT cooperation, but on the eve of the delegation's arrival, Hsaio Shu-Lin, director of the Taipei branch of UPI, announced that Henry Liu had been a KMT spy sent to the U.S.—not to spy on Chinese-Americans—but on the American government. "The News Weekly" and "Time Weekly" picked up the story; the former had found out Henry had been an Information agent, the latter revealing he had been a "three-sided spy" for Beijing, Taipei and Washington, D.C.

The reports were oddly suspect, if for no other reason that they were meticulously timed to go off with the arrival of the delegation from the U.S.; that, and the fact neither publication had reported on the Liu case before. What neither of the accounts reported was where this blockbuster information came from. it looked like a smear campaign, at first glance. Could it be that the Information Agency had created the story to ruin Henry's reputation, to quiet growing dissatisfaction with the KMT in Chinese society, and to take-some of the steam out of the pressure applied by the U.S. Congress?

In Hong Kong, a magazine called "The Nineties" published a series of seven letters purportedly written by master spy Henry Liu to a correspondent in Taipei. The only letter signed with Henry's name was the first, dated 6 February 1984, addressed to "Mr. Hsia," and the rest were signed "Hsaing-Chen" or were left blank. Nowhere did the sender's address appear, and all of the letters had been mailed to a post office box in Taipei.

The content of the seven letters was rich with information about the movements of mainland Chinese and Taiwanese in the U.S., including an analysis of their activities and certain judgments as to their purpose. The first letter, allegedly sent to Henry's mentor at "The Taiwan Daily News," contained a declaration of loyalty to the KMT government, and Henry's promise to change the biography of Jiang Jingguo, as the KMT wished. There were remembrances of how he had been sent to America as a correspondent for TDN, how his articles had created many enemies, and how those enemies had made life miserable for his publisher. Through it all, Mr. Hsia continued to support him, for which Henry was grateful, and the letter goes on to recount how Mr. Hsia had personally journeyed all the way to San Francisco from Taiwan out of concern for Henry's book about the president.

In this same letter, Henry relates that he had been away from his homeland sixteen years when, in 1980, he suddenly yearned to go back for a Visit. He remembered having spelled out to Mr. Hsia the terms and conditions under which he would make the pilgrimage: there would be no public announcement or fanfare; the KMT would foot the bill; and that President Jiang Jingguo would receive him. Analysts of this letter thought that herein lay the reason for Henry's supplying information on the movements of Chinese expatriates: he was hoping his cooperation would

bring about the approval of his trip.

"The Nineties" contacted Mr. Hsia for his explanation of the letter, which he admitted to have received. He had no idea how it fell into the hands of the Information Agency, which in turn had provided it to the magazine for publication. There were two possibilities: that the letter had been intercepted due to Henry's activities as a known spy, or that Hsia had been absorbed into the cover-up and his denial deflected responsibility. Those in the know considered the second scenario the more plausible-if the letter was authentic.

A second letter, dated 25 March 1984, was puzzling in that it seemed to be a deliberate effort to confuse its recipient. In it, Henry asks for topics for articles and targets for spying. He reports that the editing of his book on Jiang had been completed, at the behest of Mr. Hsia. He provides a tip on Kuo-Chen Wu, a Chinese government employee at odds with co-workers in the U.S., and tips on the director of the Taiwan Association and the editor-in-chief of "The Taiwanese Voice." Then the letter spins off on a mockery of a group of four sons of prominent Chinese military officials visiting the U.S. to purchase arms. The letter was signed, "Hsiang-Chen."

A third letter, unsigned and undated, bore a postmark of 18 May 1984. It was a rambling narrative of a meeting in Palo Alto, California, between the director of "Tsi-Li Evening News" and other members of the Chinese-American press community. One was Da-Jen Jung, a calligrapher, whom Henry insulted as "intolerable." Another was a woman named Fu-Mei Chang, who accused "The Nineties" of publishing immoral lies about her and her husband, that they were sponsors of the Tiawanese Independence Movement.

The publication of the letters by "The Nineties" prompted the Chinese-American media to seek out Henry's widow, Tsui, for her reaction, especially to the revelation that her husband-a scholar, journalist and shopkeep—was also a three-sided spy. "It's very funny," Tsui said, "Henry collecting information for the KMT."

Pointing to the second letter, dated 25 March, Tsui pointed out that it looked like Henry's handwriting and the content similar to the way he spoke, but the signature "Hsiang-Chen" was new to her, and an obvious fake. Somewhere in the middle of this letter—which went on for several pages—the original message from Henry to a friend in Taiwan had been supplanted with a forgery. Hence, the confusing spin-off about the group of arms merchants. Her guess was that Henry's gossipy newsletter to a pal had been altered to appear as an informant's installment to the KMT.

The chairman of the American delegation looking into the into the Liu matter, Lin-Tsi Wang, wasted no time in accusing the KMT of trying to distort the focus of the investigation by planting the letters in the media. It was obvious to Wang that the KMT was trying to foist blame on renegades in the Information Agency who had acted without authority in the Liu assassination. The appointment of Chin-Hsi Wong by the KMT to head up the Taiwanese investigation into Henry's murder was a sham, as Wong was a known KMT puppet. All these promises of cooperation from the KMT, said Wang, had failed to materialize.

"The KMT is hitting the bush to hide the truth," Wang admonished. "Justice is not being served. This is an insult to intelligence."

The KMT was unyeilding in the matter of Henry's identity as a spy. They produced a file of his Information Agency reports, and exhibited cancelled paychecks as further proof. If anyone had cause to doubt Henry's true identity, the money trail appeared most convincing.

In Henry's defense, his widow, Tsui, sat down with reporters to clear up suspicions that there was indeed more to Henry than meets the eye. "You are aware, of course, that following President Nixon's visit to China in 1972, that many Chinese visited America," Tsui began. "And you will no doubt remember that for several years it was customary for the FBI to question Chinese upon entering America. When Henry made his first return visit to China in 1975, he was interrogated at length upon his return to San Francisco. It was a matter of national security then.


So, if someone says Henry was a spy simply because he had been interrogated by the FBI, then there were many spies."

Tsui smiled, and as reporters sat quietly and took notes in two tongues, she addressed the more sensitive issues of her husband's history.

"In 1981, Henry made another trip to mainland China to research his biography of Jiang Jingguo. He visited Hsi-Kuo, the president's childhood home, in Chang-Hua, and took photographs which he sent to Jiang's brother, General Jiang Wei-Kuo, to show respect. He did not expect to receive a letter from a friend of the general thanking him, and requesting Henry to take more photographs upon his return to mainland China in future. When Henry returned the following year, he went back to HSi-Kuo and, with the assistance of Communist officials, took many photographs which he forwarded to the Jiang family in Taiwan. An assistant to the president wrote a grateful letter to Henry, expressing the family's appreciation."

Tsui sifted through the evidence piled on the desk before her. "This payment," she said, pointing to a photograph in "The Nineties" magazine, "this check that the KMT says was payment for information, was in appreciation for the photographs Henry sent the president's family."

Among the crowd of journalists, several hands shot up, a flood of questions regarding Henry's contacts with President Jiang and his family.

"During Henry's second trip, after visiting the mainland, he went to Taipei. He told many KMT officials of the photos he had given President Jiang of his childhood home, which had recently undergone renovation by the Communists. The photos were transferred to video, and Henry personally delivered the tape to the president. They watched the film together, after which Jiang said, 'The Communists have finally done one good thing for me,' and he was very happy with the way his home had been made into a shrine."

Tsui paused from her narrative to interject a personal observation. "If this account I have just related to you gentlemen adds up to 'supplying information to the government,' then no doubt Henry was considered a spy."

In follow-up questions regarding Henry's relationship with President Jiang's family, Tsui sensed that some of the writers were still not completely convinced that her husband hadn't been cooperative with the KMT, especially if he maintained a warm personal relationship with Jiang's brother.

"One thing is true," Tsui admitted, "Henry always appreciated General Jiang Wei-Kuo, the president's brother. They were friends, going back to 1960, when Henry's first child was two or three years old. The baby had a thyroid condition and needed surgery. Henry could not afford it, but General Jiang arranged for the operation at the veteran's hospital. And if the account I have just provided you also adds up to collaboration with the KMT, then my husband is guilty."

Following up on the information provided by Tsui, reporters inquired of the FBI in Washington, D.C. as to their interrogations of Henry Liu attendant to his comings and goings to China back in the Seventies. "The American Chinese News" published the FBI's response on 23 January 1985, a statement from spokesman Lane Bonner, who categorically denied that Henry had been an FBI informant.

"To say that Henry Liu was 007 is to murder him a second time," The News concluded. "It is an assassination of his character."

The rumor that Henry was a three-sided spy proved to be just that—a rumor. It was apparent that the publication of the seven letters was a KMT ploy. What no reasonable person could fathom was, how did the accusation by the KMT that Henry was a spy prove the Information Agency's innocence in his murder?

As far as observers were concerned, there were only two possible reasons for disclosing Henry's identity as a spy: first, to exonerate the KMT by creating a situation that proved he lived a dangerous life and that his killing was not a tragedy; there was no reason for the KMT to kill one of their own. Second, it blew apart the argument from U.S. congressmen that the KMT had executed an American citizen when in all actuality they were rushing to the defense of a KMT spy; the investigation of the American delegation sent to Taipei would end before it began.

However, if publishing the seven letters changed people's thinking about Henry's murder, it could also produce opposite reactions to the KMT.

If Henry, in the letters, was providing accurate reports to the Information Agency, other operatives would be threatened by the KMT's ties to Tsu-Len Gang and might reasonably fear the same fate. The KMT's silence on the matter and refusal to cooperate with the investigation was going to make it difficult to maintain relationships with Information agents in the future.

While the KMT busily tried to expose Henry as a spy by publishing his letters, they had also unwittingly admitted to operating a network of paid informers in the United States. If congress ever needed proof of the existence of spies, the Taiwanese government was offering it freely in the newspapers. In the frantic effort to absolve itself of blame in the murder of Henry Liu, the KMT was destroying diplomatic relations with the United States.

This same chain of evidence, designed by the KMT to show Henry as a bad guy who did anything for a buck, also went a long way in proving the KMT's ties to organized crime. No other reason for Henry's murder had been proffered, save his critical book about Jiang Jingguo. The only party with a complaint against Henry was the Taiwanese government, yet his killers were gangsters. There had to be a connection somewhere.

In the final analysis, the publication of the seven letters was deemed to be a poorly devised smokescreen. It didn't really matter who Henry Liu really was—scholar, spy, shopkeep or informer-all that mattered was he had been murdered, and the only reasonable explanation for it was his criticism of President Jiang Jingguo. The KMT's tactics of blaming Tsu-Len Gang, scrounging for scapegoats in the Information Agency, and finally resorting to trashing Henry's reputation had done nothing more than blaze a trail back to KMT headquarters.

The publication of Henry's letters by "The Nineties," a KMT-controlled magazine with clout among Chinese abroad, caused other publications to criticize the ploy and the KMT was forced to change tactics again. "The Nineties" editor-in-chief, Li Yi, provided a disclaimer that, as a long-time friend of Henry Liu who had printed his articles, he did not want to publish the seven letters, but disclosed their existence as a matter of responsibility to his readers. By the end of Li's column, the disclaimer had turned into a defense of the KMT, and readers saw the fine hand of the Information Agency in its true purpose.

Henry's true friends recalled that "The Nineties" had never been the supporter of Henry that Li Yi claimed to have been. They remembered Li's refusal to print any reference to Henry's biography of Jiang, not even ads for which "The Nineties" would be paid to publish. Thus, the "responsibility" Li claimed he owed the public turned out to be nothing more than an "obligation" to the KMT.

The posture of the KMT which began with an aggressive self defense now turned more offensive. The initial passivity toward the truth coupled with an intense attack on the credibility of the victim was not working. The KMT's claim that Henry had been a spy for three countries and deserved his fate was not much more effective. After killing a man it is safe to attribute all blame to him; dead men tell no tales.

The KMT had played all their cards. Resolution of Henry's murder was now left up to the U.S. Congress. All that remained was for the American fact-finding mission to do its duty.

# Chapter Nine

## Jung Tsi-Tsui

In the days and months following the murder of Henry Liu, the emotional focus of the story was bound up in his widow, Jung TSi-Tsui. "The image of Henry lying in his blood appeared in my mind day and night," she said to reporters. "Anger suppressed my sorrow, and gave me power to search for the truth."

People who knew Tsui understood how difficult it was for her to appear in public and make tearful appeals for justice. Tsui was the typical, traditional oriental woman, and an introverted wife and mother. She did not like drawing attention to herself. The death of her husband thrust her into the spotlight, and she divided her time between lawyers, journalists, investigators and what was left of the family business. Fueled by a love for her dead husband and an anger that stoked her courage, Tsui was fortified by an outpouring of concern and assistance from strangers in every walk of life who shared one idea in common: Henry Liu did not die without reason.

Tsui never had any doubt that Henry's murder was politically motivated. She said so from the start, in telephone calls home to China, Taiwan and Hong Kong. She rejected the hypotheses of Daly City police that Henry may have been the victim of a robbery gone wrong, or of blackmail due to an illicit affair. She knew her husband, she had seen his killers, she was convinced of a connection to Taiwan. And she was running out of patience with the ever-changing KMT tactics which painted Henry as a turncoat and a spy.

Getting the truth out of the KMT was like getting toothpaste from a tube: when the U.S. Congress gave a little squeeze, out came a little truth. The KMT thought that by arresting two gangsters and three high-ranking Information agents, the U.S. would go away and allow Taiwan to handle its sovereign affairs. And, as the congressional fact-finding mission to Taipei bogged down in red tape, Tsui reached the end of her patient waiting for justice to be given her. She then did something very bold, something atypical of the typical oriental housewife: she decided to sue the ROC government.

"It is said among the KMT-controlled newspapers in Taiwan that Henry's murder was a personal act of vengeance and not a national political activity," Tsui began the reasoning process to her lawyer. "If the director of the Information Agency and two top aides were involved, how is it not considered a national political activity? What would it be?"

Tsui had a point there. At least, her lawyer thought so. Believing that Old Duck and Information Agency Director Hsi-Lin Wang were mere scapegoats, Tsui convinced her lawyer to sue the entire government and let the chips fall where they may.

On 11 October 1985, Tsui filed suit against the ROC government in the Federal District Court of Northern California. She sued them for the murder of her husband, and attached a civil complaint asking for $350 million in compensation. She delivered the papers to the Clerk of Court personally.

The initial reaction from Taipei was predictable: there would be no offer of settlement, owing to the ROC's position that it was in no way, shape, manner or form responsible for Henry's death. The actions of the director of the Information Agency and his aides were acts of "individual personal behaviour," and not a national political action. If the ROC government bore any responsibility at all, it was merely of the moral kind, not a direct cause.

It would take almost two years for the American legal system to inter-face with its Taiwanese counterpart. on 27 August 1987, Judge Eugene Lynch summoned Tsui to court and advised her that, in his opinion, the judgment of the Taiwanese court was based on the facts and that the ROC government was not responsible for Henry's murder.

Tsui stood before the judge in disbelieving silence. She was frozen with anger, and the judge realized that his explanation would require further elaboration. "If the plaintiff wishes to win this case," Judge Lynch directed, "she will have to show evidence controverting the facts relied upon by the court in Taiwan. Otherwise, the judicial system in Taiwan does not follow the principles of American law."

Tsui promptly filed an appeal with the California court and, barring any new evidence, the appeal was rejected.

Tsui did not understand, but she did not give up. With the support of true friends, she filed a new appeal with the Ninth Circuit on 17 March 1988. And she waited 21 long and torturous months for the decision which aban-doned the original judgment of Eugene Lynch and directed the court to re-hear the case against the ROC. The main reason for the reversal was the legal concept that the unauthorized behaviour of an employee-in this case, Information agents—when it is within the scope of his employment, and even in the absence of knowledge by the employer (the ROC), the employer is held responsible for the actions of the employee.

On review, the court saw the facts of the case in a new light and deemed it was sufficient to show that the ROC government was responsible for the death of Henry Liu. The actions of Hsi-Lin Wang were a direct outgrowth of his position as Director of the Information Agency, and under California law, the government of Taiwan was responsible.

Lawyers representing Taiwan were not so quick to settle with Henry's widow. They had won the first case with Judge Lynch, and they had beat back the appeal. They had reason to believe that the judgment of the Ninth Circuit would also be reversed by the Supreme Court. The down-side was that a verdict for the plaintiff by the high court would necessarily include a larger settlement and would greatly embarrass the already belea-guered Taiwanese government.

The lawyers for the ROC reached a consensus: because the case was politically sensitive, no offers of settlement would be made to the plaintiff; it would be easily misunderstood. Any money paid to Henry's widow must appear in the form of comfort-not compensation—and therefore the lawyers for Taiwan suggested in a formal recommendation to the Ministry of Domestic Affairs that they wait for Tsui to come begging.

The Ministry of Domestic Affairs gathered the Directorate Governor of Budget, the Ministry of Justice, and the National Security Council for meet-ings during the first three months of 1990. The plan was to proceed on both fronts: to continue the case on appeal while entertaining any offers from the plaintiff to settle. Payment to Tsui, if any, would come in the form of a sym-pathetic gesture toward the Liu family while staunchily maintaining the gov-ernment's innocence. Payment would then only be made in exchange for Tsui's promise to end all appeals both in the U.S. and Taiwan. It was all being done in a last ditch effort to save face in America; dealing with Taiwanese tax-payers who would foot the bill would come later.

Before proceding with the plan on both fronts, the lawyers for Taiwan pointed out potential pitfalls. There were only two ways to overturn the ruling by the Ninth Circuit: by asking for a re-hearing or on an appeal to the Supreme Court; chance of success for either was slim. On the other front, the cost of settling the suit would be far less than continuing the fight, losing, and being forced to pay compensation. Any effort by Taiwan to avoid paying compensation would be enforced by the U.S. government and further damage diplomatic relations. under these circumstances, con-tinuing to fight Tsui's case yielded a diminishing return for the ROC.

The involvement of the Information Agency in Henry's murder was gen-erally accepted, the attorneys argued. The damage at home has been done. The people of Taiwan believed the nation was morally obligated to the Liu family, and payment should be made to them according to principles of humanity and justice. In doing so, the KMT told its attorneys that payment was not so simple: the Liu case did not comply with civil law; the government might dole out assistance to the Lius, but it would have to be done in the form of a special project by the Executive Yuan. The smokescreen must remain in place, at all costs; any resolution resulted in controversy.

With a collective shrug of the shoulders, the lawyers representing Taiwan left the Executive Yuan building and journeyed back to the U.S., where they informed the Office of Taiwan that they would be filing an appeal with the U.S. Supreme Court. When news of the action reached Tsui through her lawyer, she felt utterly exhausted. Six years had drained away since Henry's murder, and she did not know how much more of this she could take. offer to settle, she told her lawyer. Put an end to this madness.

The ROC filed its motion with the U.S. Supreme Court on 14 May 1990. Ten days later, attorneys for both sides met to discuss settlement. Tsui's lone lawyer looked across the table at the team representing Taiwan and made a request of $3 million in compensation for his client and an open apology. The offer was flatly rejected; Tsui couldn't get that much from the court.

Two weeks later, the attorneys for Taiwan offered Tsui $1 million in "comfort," but only on condition that she not play up the incident in the future by writing a book or making a movie. "My client won't settle for less than two million," Tsui's lawyer replied, "but I will advise her of your offer."

By the end of June, both parties agreed in principle on a settlement of $1.5 million. Words and phrases such as "no legal responsibility" and "comfort not compensation" were minced, and drafting a final resolution bogged down in legalese and doubletalk. Taiwan refused to offer an apology, and this issue alone became a sticking point.

On 19 September 1990, the Executive Yuan signed off on the agreement and forwarded $1.45 million to their office in the United States. Upon receipt of the funds on the 27th, Tsui's lawyer withdrew his case from the federal court in California at the same time Taiwan dropped its motion before the U.S. Supreme Court.

The terms of the agreement provided that the Taiwanese government was paying an amount of "exgratia instead of compensation," that it had no legal responsibility for Henry's murder. The terms were to be kept secret, and Tsui agreed not to create a book or movie about the affair.

Regarding the media and the public's right to know details of the settlement, the attorneys for Taiwan specified that the parties "can only disclose that the controversy has been solved to satisfy both sides and the plaintiff has received a great amount of comfort money from the ROC government while the ROC government denies they are responsible and the suit has been withdrawn."

While such a clause might seem reasonable under the circumstances, the ROC went further in securing its position: not only was Tsui barred from testifying in court against her husband's murderers, she was permanently barred from "stating the truth of the murder in public."

One million four hundred fifty-five thousand dollars in return for silence—that was the deal. No apologies, no admissions, no confessions in exchange for no books, no movies, testimony. The matter of Henry Liu was to be dropped.

The only losers in the case appeared to be the people of Taiwan, who paid the price and were never told how much.

# Chapter Ten

## Kuei-Sen Tung

One might reasonably expect the tragedy of Henry Liu to end with the settlement of the claim made by his widow. The matter would disappear from the newspapers, and the U.S. Congress could get back to normal relations with Taiwan. And back home, it would be business as usual: the scapegoats in the Information Agency would be restored to their former positions, and Old Duck and Wu Duen would be quietly released from prison back into the muddy stream of TsU-Len Gang. That's the way this world turns.

There were details and loose ends to tie up, however. Not everyone is accounted for. Among the missing, the most notable is Kuei-Sen Tung, the second triggerman in Henry Liu's murder.

When last this narrative concerned itself with Tung's activities, it was in the days immediately following Henry's murder. He had hesitated to return to Taiwan with Old Duck out of fear for his safety, but was prepared to accept full responsibility for Henry's murder if it meant that Old Duck would look after his family. Even though Old Duck assured Tung's safety, Old Duck had taken the precaution of depositing a copy of his taped confession with White Wolf for safe keeping.

Tung had grown up in a military family. His father was a foot soldier, and life was difficult. He graduated from military school and served ten years in the ranks. When he retired, Tung received $20,000, half of which he gave to his mother, the rest he spent on a motorcycle in order to create a delivery service.

Tung had no friends in the business world. At the start of his bright future, he soon failed.

Through an old army pal Tung met Old Duck, who put him to work in a coffee shop. Everyday life was to sleep and make coffee. Most of his customers were gangsters, whether he knew it or not. And before he knew it, Tung was indoctrinated into the Chung branch of Tsu-Len.

Through his gang connections, Tung built up a concert promotions company. He had twenty employees, and produced television specials. Just when his business turned a corner and showed a profit, Tung ran into bad luck. one of his pals came to visit, and happened to own a bulletproof vest. The police found out and arrested them both. Tung was sentenced to six months in prison for "collaboration in an act dangerous to the public." After he completed his sentence, his company was gone.

These thoughts ran through his mind on the long flight from Dallas, Texas, to Taipei, Taiwan. He hoped that having killed Henry Liu for the good of his country that Taiwan would forgive his past and grant him a fresh start, then he could do something for his old mother to fulfill filial piety.

When Tung deplaned with Old Duck and Wu Duen, he was filled with dread that he had deceived himself and walked headlong into a KMT trap. Information Agency Deputy Director Chen Hou-Men was waiting for them with a phalanx of airport security. only after the welcome dinner and the offers of reward and a position with the Agency did Tung begin to relax. And at this point in the story, we last saw Kuei-Sen Tung.

Following the dinner with Deputy Director Chen, Tung waited to hear from him regarding the Information Agency position but Chen seemed to snub him. "Keep calm," Chen said, "stay home. These are dangerous times." And then, Tung didn't hear any more from Deputy Director Chen.

Late at night on 12 November 1984, Tung received a call from a friend: "Famous Businessmen's Club" and the offices of "Hua-Mei Report" had been ransacked by police. Old Duck and five brothers had been busted in the raid.

Tung couldn't believe the news. How could it be? He called the magazine, but no answer. Then he called the club, nobody there. And now Tung knew the situation to be serious, but he had no answer for "Why?"

Tung hit the streets in search of the early edition of "The United News." He lived near their print shop, and bought a copy hot off the press. Afraid to read it, he carefully opened it up and felt faint upon seeing the headline announcing, "Project Clean-Up!"

Tung slumped below a street lamp, clutching the paper. His mind was a mess, his temples banging like a drum. He seemed to lose consciousness, and when he revived his mind filled with hatred for the double-crossing KMT bastards who had betrayed Tsu-Len Gang.

There was only one course of action for a lone foot soldier fiercely loyal to his leader: escape to the U.S., and save Old Duck. In America, Tung could go to authorities, and with the taped confession in White Wolf's hands, convince police of its truth.

With Tsu-Len's leadership behind bars, the only person Tung could turn to for help was Bi-Ju Chuo, called "Big Sister" for her expertise in arranging flight from Taiwan. Big Sister's fee was $400,000 NT, including airfare and bribery. The price was steep, but it was the only deal in town.

While waiting for Big Sister to make arrangements, Tung was like a bird frightened by a bow. He was afraid to remain at home and afraid to check into a hotel. He hid in a Taipei safehouse, never venturing out in daytime. When boredom became intolerable, he sent scouts into the streets ahead of him. If this was the life of an Information agent, he no longer dreamed of being in the Agency.

Big Sister was extremely efficient. Soon everything was prepared for Tung's escape to America. A meeting was arranged for Tung and Big Sister to exchange cash for documents, which included an official pass worn by congressmen and government officials in transit. Big Sister drove Tung to Kaohsiung Airport, and explained procedure. The pass, she told him, had been provided by the wife of a legislator who needed extra cash. Once the pass was obtained there was no problem for its bearer; application for the pass was a tangle of red tape, and that's were valuable connections were made. Upon arrival at the airport, Tung breezed through every inspection point without a problem.

At the boarding gate, Tung met a group of "friends" who had his boarding pass. It appeared to casual observers that Tung and Big Sister were there to see them off, but during an exchange of hugs and handshakes, one of the friends slipped the boarding pass to Tung as Tung handed off the official pass. Tung boarded the plane as his friend blew past exit guards wearing the official pass.

Tung felt relief as he settled in for the flight to the Philippines. Big Sister then detailed how she would obtain a Philippine passport for him and tickets to the United States. In the meanwhile, Tung was to establish contact with White Wolf and prepare him for the job of saving Old Duck.

As the plane taxied from the terminal, Tung took a long last look at his homeland thinking he would never return. Then he inspected his documents to discover that Big Sister had given him her passport.

"You've made a mistake," Tung said to Big Sister.

"No mistake," she replied. "Filipino immigration is slack. If they are looking for names, they will not recognize mine. If they are looking for faces or passport photos, flashing my passport will confuse them. Either way, you get in."

"What will you use?"

"One of these," said Big Sister, fanning a handful of passports like a deck of playing cards, all bearing her likeness but different names.

Upon arrival in the Philippines, Tung and Big Sister had no trouble passing through immigration. They checked into a Chinese-run hotel where Big Sister was known, where Tung sat around and waited for her to retrieve his Philippine passport. Later that same day, news of Project Clean-Up reached Manila. News of Old Duck's arrest was everywhere; the owner of the hotel was afraid Tung would be discovered. It would be hazardous for them both, so the hotelier took Tung home with him to hide. He told Tung to stay put and lay low, his meals would be delivered.

For two weeks, Tung waited nervously for Big Sister's return. When she failed to show up, fear of her arrest wore out Tung's welcome at the hotelier's home. He packed up his few belongings and moved to a cheap hotel in downtown Manila.

Tung was unsure of his next move, as if he were a pawn in a giant game of chess. With a murky perception of the rules of the game and not wanting to be sacrificed, he sought connections with Tsu-Len gang members operating in Manila. By now, everyone was aware of Project Clean-Up in Taiwan, and Tung was at the top of a short list of "most wanted" fugitives. He had this news on the authority of two new friends, Ah Jui and Little Liu, foot soldiers starting out in a life of crime and anxious to curry favor with Tung, who was a hero in the hall of fame of the "most wanted" list.

Late one night, Ah Jui and Little Liu burst into Tung's hotel room, roused him from bed and threw his clothes into a suitcase. "Very urgent!" was all they could manage to say. "Very, very!" Before Tung could put his shoes on the pair had pushed him out a wiadow and down a fire escape and into a waiting car.

"A guy called Wei-Min just arrived from Taiwan. He has orders to shoot you on sight," Ah Jui shouted at Tung. "He came to me, offer me the job."

"Who sent him?" Tung asked.

"Didn't ask, didn't say," Ah Jui replied.

"What did you tell him?"

"I told him I take the job," Ah Jui smiled.

For a split second, Tung wasn't sure if his friend was saving his life or leading him to Wei-Min for the slaughter.

Ah Jui repeated, "I take the job."

"What is my head worth?" Tung asked, more out of curiosity than fear. It was a trick question, and the answer would tell him if Ah Jui was truly a friend or foe: only a loyal gang member would accept an order to murder without asking about money; if money was mentioned, then loyalty goes to the highest bidder.

"Didn't ask, didn't say," was Ah Jui's reply. "All I say is I take the job."

"You've learned much in a short time, little brother," Tung said. "Only an amateur asks for money. So, where are we going?"

"You stay with us," Little Liu said. "You decide what's next."

With no time to spare, Tung devised a plan to get rid of Wei-Min. "Go back to him and say you shot me," Tung told Ah Jui. "Tell him you shot me twice. Tell him you thought I was dead, this way you look good. But say that you ran when you heard people coming. Say you heard that friends might have taken me to Thailand, that will get him off my trail."

When the story had been rehearsed, Ah Jui and Little Liu reported to Wei-Min exactly as they were told. Wei-Min was frustrated by the news.

"So, I am to return to Taiwan and say I don't know if Kuei-Sen Tung is dead or alive, in manila or Bangkok?" Wei-Min asked Ah Jui and Little Liu. "You have put me in a very difficult
position, little brothers."

Wei-Min attached a briefcase to his wrist with handcuffs, and departed for the airport without expressing thanks or offering payment. The boys weren't certain who had sent Wei-Min, but they made up their minds not to like whomever it was.

Tung spent the next month rustling up a Philippine passport and birth certificate. It cost him $3,000 U.S., and he made successful trips to Singapore and Malaysia to put some wear on the documents. He still lacked a U.S. visa, his difficulty with English standing in his way at the American consulate.

Everything Tung needed was obtained with the help of Ah Jui, whom he repaid by giving him pocket money and picking up the tab at restaurants, telling him stories of Tsu-Len Gang exploits and giving him tips on how to get ahead in the underworld. When Tung got sick, Ah Jui took care of him. They became closer than brothers.

After repeated failed attempts to get a U.S. visa in the Philippines, Ah Jui convinced Tung that they should go to Thailand, where he knew people that could obtain a U.S. visa. Tung considered two months in Manila had left him stranded when Big Sister vanished, Old Duck was still in jail and there was no sign of his release. Any chance of getting a visa in Thailand was better than hanging around Manila: sooner or later, his money or his luck would run out.

"It would be better for you if you stay here," Tung told Ah Jui. "If I can't get a visa in Thailand, I will have to do a job for money. I don't know where I will go. Maybe Japan."

"It would be better for you if I go," Ah Jui argued.

"Better for me, yes, but I can't afford you. Let me go, and I'll send for you when I can."

Tung departed for Thailand from the Philippines in the first few days of 1985. A Hong Kong newspaper reported that taped confessions regarding the murder of Henry Liu had surfaced in the United States. Tung made an urgent call to White Wolf in Los Angeles for confirmation.

"We heard you were dead," White Wolf said. "We gave the tapes to police. We told them tapes must remain secret, to save face for KMT, else we do not get Old Duck. But now news of tapes has leaked. Everyone knows. Situation is very bad."

"Big brother, what do you think I should do?" Tung asked.

"I told police here that you're dead," White Wolf said. "I told them Wei-Min killed you."

"Who sent Wei-Min, Tsu-Len or KMT?"

"The government sent him. You are the fish escaping from the net. If KMT finds out you are still alive, they will have to negotiate with you. my advice is don't do it. You end up like Old Duck and Wu Duen."

"What are my choices, big brother?" Tung asked, afraid of the answer.

"You can run for the rest of your life," he said, then after a long pause, added, "or you can turn yourself in to the U.S. embassy. They will bring you here, you make report, you can save Old Duck."

At that moment, Tung was reminded of Ah Jui and Little Liu back in Manila. Once word of Tung's existence was made known, Wei-Min and the KMT would know Ah Jui had lied about shooting Tung, and the results would be disastrous for the little brothers.

"I come to U.S. on one condition," Tung said to white wolf, "that my friends in the Philippines come with me. if U.S. guarantees their permanent status, then I make good on a full confession of the murder of Henry Liu."

"Then prepare to come to the States," White Wolf said, as if he alone had the power to grant immunity. "Of course, I must make arrangements with immigration for your friends, but you report to the nearest U.S. embassy."

Tung's fear was that dealing with one government was no different than any other. The chance of falling into a trap in America was as likely as being snared by the KMT. He knew deals could only be made at a distance; once he entered a U.S. embassy, he was on American soil and the game would be played by their rules, of which he had no knowledge.

Tung's first move was to alert his little brothers. "The choice is yours," he told Ah Jui and Little Liu, "but your choices are the same as mine. You can run, or you can flee to America."

The little brothers told Tung they would see him in Thailand very soon. Very, very.

Together again, the trio was short of money. Almost miraculously, who should arrive from Los Angeles but Yellow Bird, the Tsu-Len stateside operative. Yellow Bird was close friends with Old Duck, to whom he was steadfastly loyal, but he was also obliged to White Wolf, whom he dealt with cautiously.

Yellow Bird's arrival in Thailand was no coincidence. He knew all about Tung's plight. "If you turn yourself in to the Americans, you will be tried for murder, and there is no guarantee it will help out our friend, Old Duck. I have doubts," Yellow Bird said, and continued as if he were betraying a confidence. "White Wolf has reported you to the U.S. embassy in Philippines. They are waiting for you."

"What about them?" Tung asked, nodding at Ah Jui and Little Liu.

"They are no concern to anyone. They are nothing. They probably end up in same cell with you."

Tung found himself in the uneasy position of relying upon Yellow Bird's judgment. He seemed to know so much more about Tung's situation than Tung did. Yellow Bird reached into a pouch for straps of U.S. currency and stacked $20,000 on the table, as if he knew the solution in advance.

"Go to Dominica," Yellow Bird dictated. "I have friends there. They have a farm. You three guys can work there until things quiet down."

Yellow Bird handed Tung a slip of paper with names, numbers and addresses. With that, he gripped Tung's hand, and hugged him in a fraternal embrace.

"You did what you had to do," Yellow Bird whispered in Tung's ear. " Now you must do this."

Then Yellow Bird turned and disappeared into thin air as quickly as he had arrived.


Twenty thousand American dollars was a huge amount of money to Tung and his little brothers. They were rich. After debating White Wolf's advice to turn himself in to the U.S. embassy against Yellow Bird's suggestion that they lay low in Dominica, Tung decided that the three brothers should become farmers.

Now that White Wolf had alerted the embassy in the Philippines, it wasn't safe to book passage anywhere on a commercial airline under their real names. Tung resorted to underground connections for passports, visas and tickets at a cost of $10,000 U.S.

The remaining $10,000 was still a large sum of money for the trio. They were unaccustomed to wealth, and acted like it. They went to the races and tried to impress their friends by making lavish bets which failed to materialize at the finish line, then made the bigger mistake of entrusting the remainder of their stake in the hands of a professional gambler, a friend of Ah Jui, who guaranteed success.

"You guys don't know this track like I know this track," the gambler said, laughing. "Double your money, guaranteed."

The trio was surprised to discover that the professional gambler lost their money quicker than they did. Ah Jui was in a state of shock. Yellow Bird's plan was so enticing, and now all the money was gone. Disgraced by his friend, Ah Jui abruptly took off for his brother's home in Japan, and later disappeared in Singapore.

Tung had no choice but to try to get his money back from the gamblers. He was certain they had cheated him somehow at the track, and stood before the local ganglord who controlled off-track betting and made his complaint. Tung's identity as "most wanted" preceded him; the gang produced $6,000 in U.S currency and paid Tung out of respect.

To make up for what they lacked in ready cash, the Thai ganglord invited Tung and Little Liu to stay in his home until their papers came through. Home was little more than a shack with a concrete floor. They slept together on the floor like refugees, ate noodles every day. Then the news arrived from America that White Wolf had been arrested, and Tung knew then that White Wolf had fallen into a trap of his own design.

Tung was now the only man on earth who could save both Old Duck and White Wolf. Their indebtedness to him would be impossible to repay, and in trying, they would make Tung's family very wealthy—but at the cost of Tung sacrificing his freedom; it was expected of every loyal Tsu-Len Gang member to sacrifice himself for the gang.

A month after slinking off, Ah Jui called Tung from Singapore to say that he had met with luck and wanted to put matters straight with Tung and Little Liu. He expressed his regret for the mistake of trusting his gambler friends, and upon hearing this Tung and Little Liu softened. They agreed to meet up in Singapore, and travel together back to Thailand.

What was best for Tung was no longer best for his little brothers. Ah Jui and Little Liu would be better off in America, far away from the KMT, while Tung would be safer in Dominica, out of everyone's way. The trio decided to venture as far as Brazil together, and then go their separate ways.

In Rio de Janeiro, Tung reestablished contact with Yellow Bird in Los Angeles. Tung could tell Yellow Bird was happy with the news, even through the overseas connection. However, news of recent developments in the Henry Liu investigation was not favorable. This wasn't an opportune time for Tung to come to the United States. His efforts might not save Old Duck and Wu Duen and probably harm them too. Best if all three proceded to Dominica, as originally planned.

Two weeks later, the trio obtained visas for Dominica. They had used up most of their money, and Tung was forced to call Yellow Bird and confess the predicament of having been cheated by gamblers at a Bangkok racetrack. Tung had sold his gold watch and diamond rings, and still did not have enough for three tickets to Dominica.

Although he promised to rush to their rescue, it took Yellow Bird almost one month to reach them in Brazil. He did not come to take them to Dominica, he had changed his mind. They were all going back to the United States-but not yet. It would take another two weeks for Yellow Bird to arrange visas, and he would have to return to Houston without them for now. Yellow Bird stayed in Brazil three days, then returned to Texas, leaving the trio with enough money to live on for fourteen days.

A month passed without hearing from Yellow Bird. When money got tight, the trio found a place to stay costing ten dollars per night. When they got down to their last fifty dollars, they began to worry. Their hotel provided them a meager breakfast, from which they spirited away extra slices of bread. From the market they purchased ginger root, soya sauce and corn. And then they went to work—not making lunch—but a trap for catching pigeons.

Spreading out corn on the roof of the hotel, the trio laid traps of loosely knotted string which weren't quick enough to snare their quarry. So they set about fashioning a pot out of aluminum foil which perched precariously on a tripod of sticks above a bowl of birdfeed, and when pigeons wandered near the bowl, the sticks were jerked away and the pot fell on the pigeons. The pot was then put to the purpose of cooking pigeons. With a little ginger and soya, the trio devoured the meat like a delicacy. on a good day they caught three or four birds.

At last, the trio heard from Yellow Bird. He called to say he was arriving in a few days to bring them back with him to the United States, and then he said something that made Tung wonder: "If I don't have the time to come, I will have someone bring the visas to you." And then he hung up abruptly.

Afterwards, the trio did not get any news from Yellow Bird for awhile.

Days passed, the trio's situation grew desperate. Their money was gone, they had no place to stay. Tung put in a call to Yellow Bird in Houston.

An unidentified voice answered. "Yellow Bird has been arrested."

Tung was shocked. Ah Jui and Little Liu crowded around the receiver to hear the news.

"The FBI caught him in a trap," the voice continued. "He was trying to buy illegal passports."

Tung was afraid to ask the next question. "What happened to the photographs and signatures that were to be used on the passports?"

"FBI has them."

Tung hung up the phone. "We are in trouble," he said to his little brothers. "We are in big trouble."

"Very, very," said Little Liu.

In the days following Yellow Bird's arrest, Tung made repeated attempts to find out more information from Houston. He had trouble getting through, then was told not to call back for two weeks; code words were passed, the FBI was tapping Yellow Bird's phone.

With Old Duck, White Wolf and Yellow Bird in prison, the baton was passed to Huang Chi, a Chinese-American gangster based in New York. Tung did not know Huang Chi, but the new boss was well aware of Tung and his dilemma.

"We can't stay here," Tung said to his little brothers. "The FBI knows we're here. They've tapped the phones in Houston. They have our visa photos and signatures. We have to go."

Considering the options, Tung decided the easiest route and path of least resistance was to Paraguay. With Brazilian papers in hand, obtaining a legal visa to Paraguay was easy, but when the trio turned up at the consulate, telephone calls were clandestinely made and Brazilian police were waiting for them when they exited into the bright, hot light of day.

Tung, Ah Jui and Little Liu were led into three different offices by armed guards who relieved them of all travel documents and anything else in their possession. Although apart, the trio protested in unison: we've done nothing wrong.

Each of them was asked one question by a police interpreter: "Who is Kuei-Sen Tung?"

When the question was put to Tung, he felt faint. The police placed a document in front of Tung with his name and photo. The words were printed in English; he couldn't read it.

There was no point in hiding the truth, Tung thought. The sadness and anger welling up inside him could only be explained as "weeping without tears."

"I am Tung," he said to the interpreter. "Those two have nothing to do with me."

The interpreter searched Tung's eyes for what seemed an eternity before translating for the other officers. Ah Jui and Little Liu were turned loose.

Tung was hustled off to a detention center. The immigration officer there told him he would be sent to the United States in three days.

Two months later, sitting in this same cell in Rio, Tung figured he had been forgotten and would die in that spot of old age.

Examine thoughts. That is what the Buddhist is taught, to know one's own mind. For Tung, there was plenty of time for contemplation, and at the end of each mental exercise he recreated his mind by clearing it of all thought. He meditated on emptiness, of a sky without clouds, of an ocean without waves. He had been taught that he could purge himself of sin—even the murder of Henry Liu—by reciting the proper mantras. And he strived to remain in this state of refuge in order to shut out the misery that engulfed him in a Rio prison.

He wasn't sure how long he'd been there. At one point he was so certain he had been forgotten that he thought he might try walking out the front door like a visitor. That dream gave way to the idea of breaking out, and when that vision dissolved Tung was left with a desperate feeling only suicide could solve.

He thought of the ways to end his life, looking for anything that might do him great harm. There was nothing to hang himself with, nothing to open a vein. He tried prying the nails from the heels of his shoes, planning to swallow them and tear himself apart inside out.

At the end of his rope, Tung confessed to Father Yao, a Chinese priest who made weekly visits to the only Chinese prisoner in Rio detention. "I'm begging you, Father. Please bring me a poison so I can end this misery."

Father Yao refused. "As long as there is life, there is hope," he said.

Tung repeated Father Yao's words over and over in his mind. The word "hope" took root in his soul; if he died without explaining his part in the murder of Henry Liu, then those doublecrossing KMT bastards would win. Old Duck, White Wolf and Yellow Bird would perish, and no one would ever know the truth.

Tung's survival was not only preferable to suicide, it was of paramount importance.

Finally, guards came to the detention center to take Tung away. They spoke no Chinese; he thought he was on his way to jail in the United States. As it turned out, it was only another prison in Brazil.

Actually, the new lock-up wasn't a prison at all. It was more like a barracks. Tung had his own room, with a real bed and sheets and pillows, instead of a cot. There was a door to the room which was never locked; there were no bars. His fellow inmates included a Brazilian lawyer and a Lebanese businessman. Both of them were rich, and the prison staff were like their personal servants. "Money can make evil work for you," as the old saying goes. All in all, life wasn't so bad for the next five months that Tung wasted there.

Tung had been jailed in Brazil almost eight months before he made his first court appearance. No one had told him why he was arrested, or on what charges he was being held; no one had to tell him, he knew. His first hearing was delayed when the court erroneously provided him with a Thai interpreter who spoke no Chinese dialect. At his second hearing, Tung was provided with a Chinese interpreter who couldn't understand Portuguese.

The entire hearing passed without Tung understanding one word of what was said. People whom he had never seen before took the witness stand and talked at length, occasionally pointing at Tung when making a point. He did not take the stand; nobody asked him anything. Somewhere near the end of all this confusion, a guard dragged him to his feet and the judge said something and he was taken away to a holding cell.

A reporter from UPI sitting in on Tung's hearing gleaned enough snippets from the proceeding to send out a report that Kuei-Sen Tung was to be extradited to the United States to stand trial for smuggling heroin. As news of his confession raced around the globe, reporters who had been covering the Liu murder and recognized the name of the second triggerman in the UPI report out of Brazil flooded the court with calls for an explanation and the jail for Tung's statement.

Tung was confused. He did not know what the reporters were talking about. "Heroin? I don't know nothing about heroin!" he protested. "The report is wrong! The court is wrong!"

While reporters in the U.S. and Taiwan struggled with Tung's identity and tried to fit him in the puzzle of Henry Liu's murder, he was taken from his holding cell in manacles and shoved into the back of an armored vehicle.

He wasn't told where he was headed when police escorted him to a private plane at Sao Paulo's Guarulhos Airport; they spoke no Chinese. He wasn't certain, but Tung had an idea he was on his way to America.

# Chapter Eleven

## *Yung*

The cabin attendants on the charter flight bearing Kuei-Sen Tung to the United States thought the passenger had lost his mind. He looked at the handcuffs on his wrists as if they were made of solid gold, and seemed to enjoy the flight as if he were on an excursion in his private jet. But the beautiful world below was not for Tung any more. With the pull of a trigger, the world began to recede from him. He was in constant retreat from everything around him.

Landing on American soil, CIA agents waiting to take him into custody, Tung wasn't thinking of jail and judge and jury. He was recalling his first visit to America all those years ago, when all he wanted was to start up a nice little import-export business. The opening of the hatch brought him back to the present. For one brief moment, as he was being taken from the plane, Tung paused at the top of the ramp and breathed deeply the last sweet gust of air in a free society before being entombed in the bowels of a federal penitentiary.

Tung sat through a trial that was every bit as mystifying as the hearing in Brazil. Acting on a tip from an informant, the CIA saddled him with a false drug smuggling charge when prosecutors discovered there was no way to put Tung on trial for the Liu murder: the other suspects, Old Duck and Wu Duen, were in prison in Taiwan and unavailable to testify; there were no witnesses; and the taped confession left behind with White Wolf was inadmissable as evidence. Oddly, no one thought to ask Tung for his confession of his role in Henry's death, which he would have happily provided, if it meant freeing Old Duck.

Tung was transferred to the U.S. penitentiary at Lewisburg, Pennsylvania, on 8 January 1987. He was a model prisoner, quickly making friends and enlisting their participation in a club to practice Buddhism.

"Prison is just another place in this world," he said. "Our bodies may be locked away, but it is the perfect opportunity to free the mind."


21 February 1991

After the evening meal, Kuei-Sen Tung was enjoying a conversation with a black inmate with whom he regularly exchanged views on politics, race and religion. They came from different worlds but their experiences were similar; discrimination has a thousand faces.

No one could recall if or when the conversation turned into an argument. Around 10:30 p.m., Tung stumbled into the i-block unit officer's office clutching his chest. "They are going to kill me," he said, and fell to the floor.

The officer saw blood flowing from a wound in Tung's chest, and triggered his body alarm to summon staff assistance. Within minutes, Tung was placed on a stretcher and rushed to the prison hospital for emergency medical treatment.

At the hospital, a physician's assistant opened Tung's shirt to examine and dress the wound. While inspecting the puncture the doctor could not help but notice the extremely impressive tattoo that covered Tung's chest like body armour: the right upper chest wall was covered by a recoiling serpent, surrounded by flowers and trees. On the left, a magnificent bird with intricately defined plummage.

Tung's bloodied shirt was stripped away and an oxygen mask placed over his face. An intravenous saline solution was inserted in Tung's left arm, and at the wrist the doctor noticed a small tattoo of the Tsu-Len Gang chop. Paramedics arrived to transport him to the nearest civilian hospital, where he underwent tests and x-rays and received three pints of blood. After examination and evaluation, the medical staff at Evangelical Community Hospital determined Tung should be evacuated to Geisinger medical Clinic in Danville, to repair damage to the right atrium and ventricle chambers of the heart.

Upon arrival at Geisinger, Tung was suffering from shock and lapsed into a coma. The emergency room had previously been prepared and the operation was begun. The operation was apparently successful, but shortly thereafter Tung developed multiorgan system failure. He remained unconscious in the intensive care unit for 41 days before dying on 3 April 1991. He was alone when he died, there were no relatives at his side; he left no word for loved ones.

Tung's mother, Li-Fang Wen, and his widow, Yung-Chih Hsaio Tung, arrived from California for Tung's burial. From the moment of their arrival, their sadness was gradually replaced by anger and confusion. No one at the prison knew who stabbed Tung, and no one at the hospital could explain why he had been taken off life support and allowed to die.

Li-Fang had been arguing with doctors about the use of life support for several weeks. The doctors said Tung would never recover, but might spend years hooked up to their machines. He ran a risk of pneumonia, they said. There is no hope of recovery.

In response, Li-Fang said to the doctor something she had read in every one of her son's weekly letters he had written over the past four years: "As long as there is life, there is hope."

Nothing the doctors said could change Li-Fang's mind. Hospital administrators made frequent calls to her home to elicit her permission to remove Tung from life support, but she refused. "Actually, we really don't need your permission," an administrator told Li-Fang, "but we'd like to have it."

Li-Fang was afraid she wasn't making her wishes understood by the hospital. She was embarrassed by her accent, and so she called a Chinese-American attorney named Tao, who wasted no time in warning the hospital that removal of life support was reckless. "You are opening the door to a lawsuit," Tao told them in perfect English. "Do not send Kuei-Sen Tung to heaven."

Tung's wife, Yung-Chih, visited her husband nine days later. The nurse on duty spent an entire afternoon persuading her to pull the plug on her husband; the doctor in charge concurred.


How odd, Yung thought, that people entrusted with the care and well-being of patients should be so anxious to end the life of a 39-year-old man.

The nurse pleaded relentlessly. When she couldn't convince Yung of the practical aspects of euthanasia, she attempted to embarrass Yung's lack of mercy.

When the nurse was quite finished, Yung drew herself to her full height, and said, "I believe you are not a person of … superstition? No. Belief. A person of belief. But after Tung was stabbed, we went to many places to ask the gods. The gods say Tung can overcome this. So, please, you must help him."

The nurse made no further attempts to change Yung's mind. Yung spent the next two days at her husband's bedside to make sure all was in order, and then returned home to California.

Two days later, the same doctor was on the phone to Yung, arguing again in a hard tone. She did not understand English perfectly, but she understood enough to gather that the hospital had decided to pull Tung's life support, and that he would die within an hour.

Yung called attorney Tao immediately. Tao faxed an urgent demand to the hospital that they cease and desist, and that the family would return to Pennsylvania to take charge on 3 March. As Yung and Li-Fang prepared to leave for the airport on the 3rd, they received word from the hospital that Tung had died. There was no point in trying to save him, they said. His days were numbered. He must've been in great pain, and to pull off life support was the only humane solution.

"Humane?" Yung repeated. "He was given shots for pain. There should be no pain. Between life and death, it is still worth it to withstand pain. No, what you have done is really inhumane. What was your hurry?"

In the aftermath of Kuei-Sen Tung's death, and perhaps in a karmic way, his family was put through the same rounds of unanswered questions that had plagued the family of his victim, Henry Liu. They wanted to know who killed Tung and why. And they wanted an explanation for the hospital's actions.

As in the Liu case, the more Tung's family found out, the more concerned they became.

First, there were discrepancies between the reports filed by the prison hospital at Lewisburg, the community hospital, and the Geisinger medical Clinic in Danville. It appeared in the prison record that Tung had been airlifted immediately to a larger facility, when actually he had spent almost two hours awaiting transport.

Second, the reports from the community hospital noted that Tung was awake when he arrived and could answer questions, which controverted the attending physician's contention that Tung was unconscious.

Third, and perhaps worst of all, the prison investigation had not turned up Tung's assailant, and if they did know, they weren't telling the family. In a shakedown of Lewisburg penitentiary by a special investigator from the Federal Bureau of Prisons, two knives made from sheet metal were found. The smaller knife, with a blade measuring 5h inches long and 1/8 inch thick, had blood smears which matched Tung's blood type. No fingerprints were detected. No witnesses came forward. The investigation ended.

In the Chinese way, Yung and Li-Fang prevailed upon their congressmen to do something. And in much the same way Henry's case became a national issue, Taiwanese politicians were calling upon the ROC to explain the death of Kuei-Sen Tung.

Tung's champion was Shao-Kang Chau, who pressed for an investigation into the murder expecting the ROC government to take responsibility. In his statements before the legislature, Chau reminded his fellows of the tragedy of Henry Liu's death some seven years ago. He reminded them that of all the people arrested and sentenced for the murder—Old Duck, White Wolf, Wu Duen and the others-all had been released from prison within five years with the exception of Kuei-Sen Tung. None had been extradited, with the exception of Kuei-Sen Tung. And none had been killed, with the exception of Kuei-Sen Tung.

As with his other co-conspirators, Tung had received orders from the Information Agency to kill Liu, Chau argued. Tung was a government agent, and the government should be concerned with his death in an American prison. As a mere citizen of Taiwan, he was entitled to no less.

Chau then turned the legislature's attention to other sensitive subjects-the payment of comfort money to the Liu family. Was Tung's family not entitled to some form of comfort?

"Keui-Sen Tung died for the Information Agency!" Chau shouted at the assembly. "The government should order our office in the U.S. to investigate, and to lend every assistance to Tung's family, for moral reasons, if for no other."

The ROC reaction to Chau's plea on behalf of Tung's family was indifferent. The matter was handed off to the Ministry of Justice. In America, the Taiwanese delegation did not even want to provide Tung's family with an interpreter.

The only form of consolation and regret came from Tsu-Len Gang. In his letter of condolence to Yung, White Wolf wrote "upon hearing of Tung's death, my whole self sunk. A man of courage leaves his somber mother, helpless wife and young child in such an unclear way."

"Odd how his involvement in Liu's murder was the least but his fate the worst," said Old Duck. "Had he not chosen exile, he would be regarded a hero like the rest of us."

Yellow Bird also contributed this observation: "Tung was the most naive and so he suffered the most. He always believed he was working for the good of his country. He could not understand why his country did not save him. Until the day he died, he held on to that hope."

Old Duck put the matter into final perspective. "We told him to do something for our country. We told him we would save him. But it was basically a political issue. Only the government could save him."

1 April 1991

To settle the matter, to bring rest to a troubled soul, a most remarkable meeting took place: the widow of Tung's victim, Tsui, invited the soon-to-be-widowed wife of Henry's murderer, Yung, to the Liu home in Daly City. Their meeting was oddly familiar instead of edgy; there is a special bond between women whose husbands have been murdered. Yung brought Tsui a gift of white flowers, and Tung's sister, Mei, gave her a box of the finest Jasmine incense.

Kuei-Sen Tung was still bound to Henry's house. Madame Chu had no trouble making contact. Her eyes half closed, her head jerking as if she were fighting off sleep, she announced that Tung was with them here and now.

Mei jumped up from her seat and frantically searched about the room for her brother. "You must return to your body," she shouted. "We have prayed to the gods, and they have promised to help… but you must wish to live!"

Tung's answer was the same as before. "He says if he goes back and recovers, it will only be temporary," Madame Chu related. "He still has to leave."

Yung began to cry. "What can we do?" she implored.

Madame Chu was having a difficult time understanding Tung's instructions. "Examine his body, he says. He was poisoned before he was stabbed."


Yung stared at Mei in disbelief. The doctors hadn't mentioned the detection of poison in Tung's blood, and he had been in intensive care more than five weeks.

"What else can we do?" Yung repeated. "Does he want to see his mother?"

Madame Chu shook her head. "No," she said. "He doesn't want to upset her. He doesn't want her to see him like this."

"But she wants to come," Yung argued with Tung's spirit.

"The answer is still no," said Madame Chu. "He is very swollen from lying in bed so long."

Silence descended upon the gathering. Yung sat by helplessly while her husband moved to and fro, from this world to the next, tired of living but scared of dying. Tears rolled down her face, and Tsui had the sudden urge to embrace her.

"Hurry," Madame Chu cautioned Yung. "He is leaving, and we may not have this chance again."

There was only one remaining unanswered question. "Kuei, who did this to you?"

The answer apparently was a long time coming. "I am only getting initials," said Madame Chu. "He doesn't know the name."

"What are the initials?"

Madame Chu listened intently, and then slowly repeated the answer from Tung. "The one who tied the knot is...K...M...T."

Kuei-Sen Tung was gone. He would not trouble Tsui again, or disrupt the Liu household. The most sorrowful person he left behind was his mother; how strange, that on the day she planned to visit her son that he died, as if he did not want her to see the sad and cruel scene.

The most regretful person was Tung's brother, who would never be able to avenge his death. But the most relieved person was the One Who Tied the Knot. He would tell people: the murder is done, everybody should look forward.

The One Who Tied the Knot never thought of taking responsibility for Tung's death because he did not plunge the knife into Tung's heart with his own hand. No one knew of his existence when Tung escaped from Project Clean-Up in Taipei. And when Tung was arrested in Brazil, the ROC made no effort to help him. Instead, they provided the U.S. with his criminal record in facilitating the sentencing phase of his trial on the trumped up smuggling charge. The ROC made no attempt to negotiate a reduced sentence for Tung, and it was their position that he should die because he had run away.

In putting the story of Henry Liu in final perspective, the Taiwanese press summed the case this way: Henry Liu was a three-sided spy who brought about his own death through his antagonism of President Jiang Jingguo; Old Duck and Wu Duen were national heroes, and Kuei-Sen Tung, why, he was a hero, too. Except he had the grave misfortune to have fallen into the hands of the Americans.

When speaking of the Liu affair, Taiwanese pundits speak of the Theory of the Three Dangs: "A fool (Ben Dang), had a gang of assholes (Hun Dang) kill a bad guy (Huai Dang)." And then they laugh out loud.

The mother of Kuei-Sen Tung appeared at a gathering of family and friends. In her small, bony hands she held an 18th century blue and white porcelain jar, the cylindrical body painted with a vivid scene of a powerful dragon in pursuit of a flaming pearl. The outside of the jar was coated with a fragile, finely cracked creamy white glaze. Inside were the grey ashes of her son.

"It is tragic that a mother with white hair sends off her son with black hair," she said. "I want to know the name of my son's killer. I want to know why he was killed. I want answers."

As the old proverb says, "Maybe it is left to the spirits to make further explanation."

# *Afterword*

The murder of Henry Liu helped the people of Taiwan understand the secret workings of their government, and allowed the people of the United States to see through the facade of the Kuomintang to its dark side.

Fearing the political storm caused by Henry's murder and the reaction of U.S. congressmen indicating a negative impact on relations with Taiwan, the KMT intended to debase Henry as a spy. True or false, one basic fact cannot be covered: A U.S citizen was murdered on American soil by Taiwanese Information agents. Intended as a smokescreen to undermine support for Henry, the ploy exposed the underhanded treachery of the ROC government, and the more they tried to wipe it out the darker it became.

The murder of Henry Liu had long-lasting effects on the Chinese-American population. whereas intellectuals thought they had the freedom of speech in America, the failure of the U.S. government to move swiftly and decisively caused many to keep their silence. Not many immigrants have the courage to protest in public the atrocity of political assassination when there appears to be no safeguard of the same fate befalling the protester. Speaking out may be better than doing nothing, but of the 400 people attending Henry's funeral, only one mourner consented to have his name disclosed to the public, a Berkeley professor named Lin-Chi Wang. An east coast memorial service for Henry was kept secret from the media out of fear of retribution.

After the mourning period, as regret turned into anger, a committee of concerned Chinese-Americans formed to pressure their representatives in Congress to launch an investigation and stand up for the rights of minorities. Even then, members of the committee were afraid to make their identities known, preferring to hide behind their spokesperson, Professor

Lin-Chi Wang. The professor was from Hong Kong, and had no relationship with Taiwan; his exposure was less than the Taiwanese-American committee members.

His powerful connections in Hong Kong enabled Professor Wang to capture front-page coverage of Henry's murder in Hong Kong newspapers. The KMT-controlled "Hong Kong Times" countered with an editorial that Henry had been killed by Communists, but in breaking their silence on the assassination, the KMT opened itself up to scathing attacks from the left.

When the investigation of California police and the FBI turned up Tsu-Len Gang's involvement in Henry's murder, the KMT reacted with Project Clean-Up, arresting ganglord Old Duck and one of the triggermen, Wu Duen, and while the KMT was quick to identify Henry's killers, at no time was a motive provided and the Taiwanese government refused to extradite the killers to the United States for trial.

The surfacing of Old Duck's taped confession forced the KMT to find a scapegoat. They gave up Information Agency Director Hsi-Lin Wang, Vice Director I-Ming Hu, and Deputy Director Chen Hou-Men, and the appearance was that the Taiwanese government was cleaning house. Actually, by arresting the Information Agency top brass, the KMT admitted the plot outlined by Old Duck was indeed true, that the Agency and Tsu-Len Gang were practically one and the same.

Beyond cancelling arms shipments to Taiwan, the government of the United States was ineffective in bringing the conspiracy to justice. Professor Wang and the Association for Chinese Human Rights in San Francisco convinced the ACLU to join them in demanding satisfaction from both the Taiwanese and American governments. Professor Wang collected the works of Henry Liu into a book designed to heighten interest in the case by allowing readers here and abroad to learn exactly which principles he died for, that his blood should not have been wasted. The inability to turn Liu's biography of Jiang Jingguo into a bestseller was perhaps the clearest indication that Professor Wang was not getting Henry's message across to the American public.

Inevitably, the murder of Henry Liu would never be resolved. The fear of Chinese-Americans coupled with the lack of concern of mainstream Americans spelled doom. Even in Taiwan, where it was pointed out that Henry Liu was born on the mainland and not Taiwanese by birth, impacted on support for his cause. The popular base on which Professor Wang tried to build his case never came together; he is to be appreciated for his efforts all the more.

If there is any moral to Henry's story for Americans, it exists to show the Kuomintang for what it really is. Since the escape to Taiwan in 1949, the KMT has portrayed itself as revolutionaries striving against Communism, the party of freedom and democracy. The image of Jiang Jieshi has been installed at the end of a long line of traditional saints, including Confucius. His son, Jiang Jingguo, is looked upon as a great leader. And these images are preserved through censorship, and where it fails—such as in Henry's case—the KMT is quick to resort to force.

If nothing else, the murder of Henry Liu exposed the collaboration between the KMT and the underworld. At last, the reason why so many criminal cases in Taiwan go unresolved is known; that the leader of a notorious gang is absorbed into the government's intelligence system is a horrifying concept for freedom-loving people everywhere.

Today, Taiwan calls itself a country of liberty, justice and democracy. The government has gone to great lengths to overcome the image of a police state, even when it admits limits to its concept of freedom. Reflecting the age-old concepts embraced by the leaders who delivered the KMT out of the mainland in 1949, today's Taiwanese government rules through the military. As long as the common people can afford rice and noodles, they dare not concern themselves with politics.

Freedom and basic rights have been whittled away in recent years. In Spring 1984, the KMT put 30 off-party publications out of business. Free speech, it seems, is free to exist as long as it conforms to the KMT party line.

In January 1991, seven years after Henry Liu's murder, when news of the investigation had ceased to air, the life sentences of Old Duck, Wu Duen and Information Agency Director Hsi-Lin Wang were commuted and they were released from prison to resume their lives precisely where they had left off. Their pardon was timed with the completion of negotiations with the Liu family, which provided that no one could speak of these matters publicly. With this final stroke of a pen on a check for $1.45 million, from the ROC to widow Liu, the KMT had effectually paid for the murder it had conspired to commit.

It is believed by Chinese-Americans that only through constant effort can liberty and democracy survive in Taiwan. They watch and wait for a new generation of intellectuals to emerge—writers with the same spirit as Henry Liu—to rise up, to fight for their own rights.

We pray Henry's blood is not wasted. We pray he will have peace beneath the soil.


END

# *About The Author*

Dr. George K. F. Wang is an eminently qualified international lawyer, professor and human rights advocate. He is a specialist in Immigration law, practicing for more than 32 years. He is chief counsel for the U.S. military before Chinese courts, and legal advisor to the governor of Yunnan province as well as many congressmen here and abroad.

Dr. Wang has lectured at National Taiwan University, Taipei College of Technology, Chung Yuen Science & Christian College, The Cultural Institute of China, Shih Chen College of Home Economics, Tamkang College of Arts and Science, National College of Art, Political Staff College, and Police officers College. He holds the position of visiting professor at Korea National University, Yunnan Industrial University, Shen Yang Industrial University, and Chin Hua University Law School in Beijing.

Dr. Wang is chief legal advisor for Taipei municipal Police Headquarters, Independent Evening News, Democratic Tau Yuan Progressive Party, Combined Service Forces R.O.C., Chung Shan Institute of Science & Technology, ministry of National Defense, China Democratic and United Party, and the Mormon Churches of Taiwan.

Dr. Wang is legal advisor to the Hon. Li-Fu Chen, founder of Chung Tung, The Investigation & Statistics Bureau of R.O.C. Kuomintang Central Execution Law Committee. He also serves as counsel to R.O.C. Premier Pei Tren Hou, and advisor to General Jiang Wei-kuo (son of Jiang Jieshi, the late R.O.C. president).

Dr. Wang is chairman of-the Dr. Sun Yixian International Foundation.

Dr. Wang is professor and representative in China of Pittsburg State University.

His many active memberships include the Taiwan Bar Association, American Bar Association, U.S. Republicans Abroad, U.S Republican

National Committee Ambassador Club, The U.S. Senatorial Club, Kiwanis, Lions, Rotary, Scottish Rite Free Masonry, Prince Hall Masons & Eastern Stars. Dr. Wang is president and chairman of Taipei, Sung Shan and Yuan Shan Lions Clubs, vice president of the Investment Association of R.O.C., and president of the Chinese American Association of the United States of America.

Dr. Wang holds the LL.B, LL.M, LL.D and PhD degrees.

A scholarship in his name has been established at Chin Hua University Law School, Beijing.

0-595-14907-3